INTRODUCTION TO HOUSE HACKING REAL ESTATE INVESTING

THE REAL ESTATE INVESTING
M E N T O R
THE AFFORDABLE $50K COACHING ALTERNATIVE

James Orr
The Real Estate Financial Planner™

Published by:

Real Estate Financial Planner LLC
PO Box 2163
Loveland CO 80539

https://RealEstateFinancialPlanner.com

First edition November 2024.
File: 2024-11-10 - Introduction to House Hacking Real Estate Investing

This publication is designed to provide accurate and authoritative information regarding the subject matter covered. It is sold with the understanding that the publisher is not engaged in rendering legal, accounting or other professional advice or services. If legal advice or other expert advice is required, the services of a competent professional person should be sought.

From a *Declaration of Principles* jointly adopted by a Committee of American Bar Association and a Committee of Publishers and Associations.

This is a work of fiction. References to clients in this book are fictional and have been modified and changed from any possible real situations to protect the identities of clients and to simplify the stories for clarity. In some cases, significant parts of the stories have been changed. In some cases, stories have been completely fabricated to illustrate a concept. Any similarities to people alive or dead is purely coincidental.

AI Disclosure: While James Orr authored the original version of this content, AI was used extensively to draft, proofread, edit, improve and write subsequent versions and variations.

DEDICATION

Dedicated to my wife Tammy. I have no words.

FREE DOWNLOAD

The World's Greatest Real Estate Deal Analysis Spreadsheet™

Thank you for purchasing this book and taking the next step toward mastering real estate investing.

As a special bonus, you can download *The World's Greatest Real Estate Deal Analysis Spreadsheet*™ for free. This powerful tool will help you analyze deals like a pro, ensuring you make informed, profitable decisions.

Download your free copy now and start running the numbers with confidence.

https://REFP.com/spreadsheet

Table of Contents

iv

Introduction to House Hacking Real Estate Investing

House hacking helps investors build wealth and live for free (or close to it). It's like the Nomad™ real estate investing strategy in that both utilize owner-occupant purchases, but they are fundamentally different.

So, what exactly is house hacking? You buy a property, live in one part of it, and rent out the rest.

This approach allows you to potentially cover your mortgage and living expenses with rental income.

Mathematically, it's like getting a side hustle that produces extra income from renting out part of your property.

- You can live for free or drastically reduce your housing costs

- Your tenants help you build equity in your property by assisting with paying the mortgage
- You can take advantage of low or no down payment and low mortgage interest rate owner-occupant financing options
- It's a great way to start your real estate investing journey
- It can help you afford a more expensive asset than you might otherwise be able to support
- You could potentially own larger assets with the limited fixed-rate loan spots, which can result in higher net worth

With house hacking you could buy a single-family home with an Accessory Dwelling Unit (ADU), a duplex, triplex, or even a fourplex.

Let's do a deep dive into house hacking.

House Hacking Variations

House hacking is a versatile strategy that comes in several variations like:

Traditional House Hacking

This is the classic approach to house hacking.

- **Down payment** - You can often get started with as little as 0% (USDA or VA), 3% conventional financing for first time home buyers, 3.5% FHA financing, or 5% down conventional financing.

- **Single Family Homes with Roommates** - This is the simplest form of house hacking. You buy a single-family home, condo or townhome and rent out spare bedrooms to cover your mortgage.
- **Duplexes, Triplexes, Fourplexes** - These multi-unit properties are excellent for house hacking. You live in one unit and rent out the others.
  - Remember, you could also add roommates to your unit for even more income. Just be aware that it's slightly harder to buy multiple properties of this type with low down payment owner-occupant financing.
  - Don't overlook non-conforming duplexes, triplexes, or fourplexes. These are properties that look like single-family homes but have multiple units. An example would be a mother-in-law basement unit that feels like a up-down duplex, but is only technically zoned single family home.
- **Additional Dwelling Units (ADUs)** - These are separate living spaces on the same property as a single-family home.

Nomad™ with House Hacking

This strategy, also known as sequential house hacking, combines the Nomad™ real estate investing strategy with house hacking.

Here's how it works:

- You buy a property and house hack it for at least a year. This is a requirement of most lenders to get an owner-occupant loan. If it takes you longer to save up a down payment for the next property, that's fine too.
- Then, you move out and rent the property you were living in. Often you rent out the entire house to one party although you could continue to rent it to individual roommates and rent it by the room.
- You repeat this process, buying a new property each year.

This approach allows you to build a portfolio of rental properties with low or no down payment and low owner-occupant mortgage interest rates while minimizing your living expenses along the way.

Check out the *Introduction to Nomad™ Real Estate Investing* book in *The Real Estate Investing Mentor* series for more information on the Nomad™ real estate investing strategy.

House Hacking with Traditional Buy and Hold

In this variation, you're not just thinking about house hacking - you're also acquiring additional properties for your real estate portfolio. While you're living in your house hack property, you're also investing in traditional buy and hold properties at the same time, in parallel.

This dual strategy can help you:

- Maximize your investment potential by diversifying your portfolio
- Add additional units faster than you could with the just house hacking and the one-year occupancy limitation
- Build equity in multiple properties simultaneously
- Learn the ropes of being a landlord in different scenarios

An example of this strategy is you own and live in a duplex with a tenant living in the second unit. Then, you also purchase additional rental properties with non-owner-occupant (investor) financing while you are house hacking the duplex.

Check out the *Introduction to Buy and Hold Real Estate Investing* book in *The Real Estate Investing Mentor* series for more information on the traditional buy and hold real estate investing strategy.

House Hacking with Short-Term Rentals

Instead of renting out your property to roommates or "unit-mate" (if you have a duplex, triplex or fourplex) you rent it out by the night as a short-term rental instead.

Here's the gist:

- You live in part of the property.
- You rent out some or all the rest as a short-term rental.

This can potentially generate more income than traditional long-term rentals, but it also requires more active management.

Check out the *Introduction to Short-Term Rental Real Estate Investing* book in *The Real Estate Investing Mentor* series for more information on the short-term rental real estate investing strategy.

Financing House Hacking

When it comes to financing your house hack, you have several options available.

Let's explore the most common strategies and a few less conventional approaches.

Traditional Owner-Occupant Loans

These are some of the more common financing strategies for house hacking:

- **Conventional Loans** - Available with as little as 3% for first time home buyers or, more commonly, 5% down payments.
- **FHA Loans** - Require a 3.5% down payment and are more lenient on credit scores.
- **VA Loans** - Offer 0% down payment options for eligible veterans and active-duty military.
- **USDA Loans** - Provide 0% down payment options for properties in eligible rural areas, but there are

significant restrictions on using USDA loans with tenants, so it is not a popular choice for house hackers.

With low down payment options, you'll typically need Private Mortgage Insurance (PMI) or something that functions like PMI (like the VA funding fee). PMI is required when you put less than 20% down when buying a property. It is insurance that you pay for to protect the lender in case you default.

While this adds to your monthly costs, it allows you to enter the market sooner and is mathematically like financing part of your down payment over time.

Less Common Financing Methods

Here are some of the less common, more unusual financing methods for house hackers:

- **Conventional Financing with Larger Down Payments** – You don't have to put down the minimum amount. You can choose to put down more which often leads to better loan-to-values which lenders reward with lower mortgage interest rates and lower PMI payments. If you put at least 20% down you can eliminate PMI altogether.
- **Loan Assumption** - Taking over the seller's existing mortgage, which can be advantageous in certain market conditions like when interest rates were low and are not much higher.
- **Owner Financing** - The seller acts as the lender, which can offer flexibility in terms and qualifications.

Holding

When it comes to house hacking, it's best described as a neutral strategy - not completely passive, but not super active either.

Let's break down the different variations and see where they fall on the active-passive spectrum:

- **Traditional House Hack** - This is generally neutral. You live in one part of the property and rent out the rest. While you're responsible for finding tenants and maintenance, it's less demanding than some other real estate strategies.
- **Nomad™ with House Hacking** - This leans slightly more active. You'll be moving yearly (or so) to a new house hack, requiring more frequent property transitions and tenant turnovers.
- **House Hacking with Traditional Buy and Hold** - This is slightly more active than just traditional house hacking. You're managing your house hack plus adding and managing additional rental properties, increasing your overall workload.
- **House Hacking with Short-Term Rentals** - This is on the more active side. You'll need to handle frequent guest turnovers, cleaning, and constant marketing of your property.

Duration

All the variations of house hacking tends to hold properties for the long term—often 20+ years to forever.

While the goal is typically to hold indefinitely, some house hackers may choose to sell or refinance to leverage up their equity.

Implementing this strategy allows you to take larger positions in the market and potentially increase your returns.

Something else to consider is as you approach retirement, you might choose to simplify your portfolio. This could mean selling some properties to focus on fewer, but better cash-flowing assets. The idea is to reduce active work while still maintaining a steady income stream.

Exit Channels

While house hackers often aim to hold properties indefinitely, there may come a time when you decide to exit your investment.

Here are the most common ways you can exit your house hack:

- **Hold Forever** - Many house hackers choose to keep their properties long-term. This allows you to continue benefiting from rental income and potential appreciation.
- **Multiple Listing Service (MLS)** - If you decide to sell, listing your property on the MLS through a real estate agent is a popular choice. This method exposes your

property to the widest audience of potential buyers, and this increased exposure often leads to maximizing price.

- **For Sale By Owner (FSBO)** - You might choose to market and sell the property yourself. While this can save on agent commissions, it requires more time and effort on your part. A popular version of this for house hackers is to sell their property as a rent-to-own to a tenant-buyer.
- **Auction** - Selling your property through a public auction can be a quick way to exit. This method might attract competitive bidding, potentially leading to a higher sale price.

While not a marketing channel itself, utilizing a 1031 tax deferred exchange allows you to defer capital gains taxes and depreciation recapture taxes by reinvesting the proceeds into another "like-kind" property. It's a great way to upgrade your portfolio without a hefty tax bill.

Check out *Should I Sell My Rental Property?* in *The Real Estate Investing Mentor* series for more information on the calculations and considerations for selling rental properties.

Exit Financing

As a house hacker, you might never want to sell your property. After all, it generates income and likely appreciating in value.

But if you do decide to exit, here are some of the more common financing options your buyers might use:

- **Traditional Owner-Occupant Loans** - If you're selling to someone who plans to live in the property, they might use conventional mortgages, FHA loans, or VA loans. These often come with lower down payments and better terms.
- **Traditional Non-Owner-Occupant Loans** - Investors buying your property as a rental typically need a 20-25% down payment. They could do it with as little as 15% down with PMI. Non-owner-occupant loans usually have slightly higher interest rates than owner-occupant loans.
- **Cash** - Some buyers, especially investors, might offer cash. This can lead to a faster, smoother closing process.
- **Rent-To-Own** - While most creative financing options aren't typical for house hack exits, you could consider a rent-to-own option. This allows you to exit more slowly and potentially reduce selling expenses. Ultimately, your buyer will likely utilize one of the other financing options we just discussed after the rental period of the rent-to-own.

Remember, you don't need to stress about how your buyer finances the purchase. However, understanding these options can help you navigate the selling process more effectively.

Investor/Entrepreneur

- Real Estate Investors tend to invest money with the hope of getting a return on that money.

- Real Estate Entrepreneurs tend to invest their time—and maybe a little bit of money—with the hope of getting a return on their time and money.

So, where does each variation of house hacking typically fall on that continuum?

- **Traditional House Hack** - This leans more towards investing money. You're primarily investing in a property with the hope of getting a return, while also reducing your living expenses. However, you'll still need to invest some time managing roommates or tenants.
- **Nomad™ with House Hacking** - This strategy requires both money and a little more time investment. You're investing in properties annually, but you're also dedicating time to move and set up new living arrangements each year. Plus, you're house hacking and managing your roommates/tenants.
- **House Hacking with Traditional Buy and Hold** - This approach is primarily about investing money. You're building a portfolio of properties, starting with your house hack.
- **House Hacking with Short-Term Rentals** - This leans more towards real estate entrepreneurship. While you're investing money in the property, you're also investing significant time in managing bookings, guest experiences, and property maintenance.

It's important to note that you can make many of these strategies more passive by building a team. For example, you could hire a property management company for your units. This can make entrepreneurial strategies look more like passive investments.

However, remember that even with a team in place, you'll still need to manage that team. This adds another layer of activity to your investment. You're not just managing properties anymore, but also people.

Money Required

When it comes to house hacking, the money you'll need to get started can vary.

Let's break down the most common and some less common costs you might encounter.

Most Common

- **Down Payment** - House hacking often allows for lower down payments compared to other real estate investing strategies. For example, you could be looking at 0% (USDA and VA loans), 3% conventional for first-time home buyers, 3.5% FHA loans, or 5% down conventional financing, depending on the loan program you qualify for and opt to utilize.
- **Closing Costs** - These are the fees associated with finalizing your mortgage. They typically range from 2-5% of the purchase price. This covers things like appraisal fees, title insurance, and attorney fees.
- **Rent Ready Costs** - This is money used to get the property ready to rent. This could range from a few

hundred to several thousand dollars, depending on the property's condition and what you're doing to rent it. For example, renting it as a short-term rental usually has higher rent ready costs since you're likely furnishing the property.

- **Cumulative Negative Cash Flow** - This is money you set aside to cover any negative cash flow you expect to see from your property until rents increase enough so you don't have negative cash flow anymore. If you put more down, you wouldn't have negative cash flow so negative cash flow is really deferred or financed down payment. It is often a smaller amount to set aside the amount of cumulative negative cash flow then it would be to set aside more down payment to eliminate negative cash flow.
- **Reserves** - It's wise to have at least six months of all expenses including mortgage payments, property taxes, insurance, HOA fees, and maintenance set aside.

Less Common

Here is some less common money required when house hacking:

- **Lease-Option Deposits** - If you're combining house hacking with the *Nomad™ with Lease-Options* strategy, you might receive non-refundable deposits from properties you're moving out of as down payments you can use toward purchasing your next property. The *Nomad™ with Lease-Options* strategy allows for unlimited down payments by using the previous property as the source of the down payment for each subsequent new property purchase.

- **Down Payment Rebates** - With the Ultimate Real Estate Agent Retirement Plan™, you might be able to get rebates on your down payments via your real estate commission.
- **Larger Down Payments or All-Cash Purchases** - While less common for house hacking, putting more money down or buying all-cash can improve your cash flow by eliminating/reducing PMI, borrowing less and improving your interest rate.
- **Second Home Down Payment** - Particularly for *House Hacking with Short-Term Rentals*, you might be able to use a 10% down payment for a second home loan.

Credit Required

When house hacking, your credit score is important, but the requirements are often more lenient than traditional non-owner-occupant investor loans. That's because you'll typically be qualifying for owner-occupant financing.

WARNING: You must move into the property, or you're committing loan fraud. Most lenders require you to live there for at least a year based on the document you sign at closing.

The typical credit score needed for house hacking is around 620.

- Some exceptions may allow scores as low as 580 (for FHA or VA loans).
- Better credit often means better interest rates and lower Private Mortgage Insurance (PMI).
- If you're buying without a loan (all cash), your credit score doesn't matter at all.

Don't worry if your credit isn't perfect. You have some options:

- Work on improving your credit score. It takes time but pays off in the long run.
- Utilize loans you can get with lower credit scores like FHA loans.
- Consider bringing in a partner with good credit. They could qualify for the loan while you manage other aspects.

Remember, even if you go the partner route or pay cash, it's still smart to work on your credit. A strong credit score gives you more options and potentially better terms in the future.

IMPORTANT NOTE: Credit score requirements can change over time, so check with your local lender for the most up-to-date credit requirements.

Using Roommate Income to Qualify for Loans

House hackers can utilize income for roommates to qualify for loans.

Fannie Mae treats rental income differently depending on whether it's from your principal residence or another property.

For your principal residence (where you're house hacking):

- The rental income from your roommates is added to your total monthly income.
- The full mortgage payment (PITIA - Principal, Interest, Taxes, Insurance, and Association dues) is included in your monthly obligations.

This means the income from your roommates can help you qualify for a larger loan by increasing your total income.

For other rental properties:

- If the rental income minus the full PITIA is positive, it's added to your total monthly income.
- If it's negative, the amount of the loss is added to your monthly obligations.

So, what does this mean for you as a house hacker?

- **Increased Buying Power** - The rental income from your roommates can help you qualify for a larger loan or a more expensive property.
- **Better Debt-to-Income Ratio** - By adding the rental income to your total income, you may improve your debt-to-income ratio, making it easier to qualify for loans.
- **Easier Qualification** - If you're struggling to qualify for a loan based on your income alone, the additional rental income could make the difference.

Here's a quick example:

Let's say you're buying a $300,000 house and plan to rent out two rooms for $500 each. Your monthly mortgage payment (PITIA) is $1,800. When applying for the loan, you can add $1,000 to your monthly income. If you make $5,000 a month from your job, your total income for loan qualification would be $6,000.

Remember, lenders will want to see that this rental income is likely to continue. Be prepared to show signed lease agreements or a history of rent payments from your roommates.

This is not a strategy just for existing homeowners. You can utilize the strategy of counting roommate income even before you own a property.

Here's an example of how that might work:

You *rent* a 4-bedroom apartment (or house). You sub-lease 1,2 or 3 of the bedrooms to roommates. This sub-lease income now counts toward your income (as described above) to qualify when you go to *buy* a property if you're taking your roommates with you to the new property you're buying and there is a lease in place.

Skills Required

House hacking requires a diverse set of skills, but you don't need to be an expert in everything from day one.

Let's break down the essential skills you'll need:

Core Skills

- **Deal Analysis** - You'll need to evaluate properties and crunch numbers to find profitable opportunities.
- **Finding Cash Flowing Deals** - You'll need to identify properties that will have strong cash flow characteristics. Ideally properties with positive cash flow, or if you're unable to find those with reasonable down payments in your market at least properties that have the least negative cash flow characteristics.
- **Acquisition Financing** - You'll need to learn how to navigate mortgages, interest rates, and maybe even some creative financing strategies.
- **Property Management** - This can vary based on your approach:

  - **Self-Managed** - You'll be the one handling tenant screening, maintenance, and rent collection.
  - **Hiring Property Management** - This can be tricky for house hacks, as many companies aren't keen on managing individual rooms. If you do find a property manager to do this, you'll need the skills of managing your property manager.
  - **Short-term Rentals** - You'll need to develop the skills for running and managing a short-term rental.

Strategy-Specific Skills

Depending on your house hacking flavor, you might need to add these skills:

- **Nomad™ with House Hacking** - You'll need to move each year and setting up new living arrangements.
- **House Hacking with Lease-Options** - You'll need to learn the lease-option paperwork that you get from an attorney and how to analyze and structure these types of agreements.
- **House Hacking with Short-Term Rentals** - Beyond marketing and hosting skills, you'll need to navigate local regulations.
- **House Hacking with Traditional Buy and Hold** - You'll need all the skills for acquiring traditional buy and hold properties in addition to your house hacking skills. The good news is that many of the skills overlap.

Stability

Shane Parrish, a renowned thinker and writer on decision-making and mental models, introduced the concept of active and passive stability in systems thinking. This idea is particularly relevant to real estate investing, including house hacking.

In the world of real estate, most strategies, including house hacking, are actively stable. This means you'll need to put in consistent effort to keep your investments performing well.

Let's break down how this applies to different house hacking variations:

- **Traditional House Hacking** - Actively stable. You'll need to manage tenants, maintain the property, and adjust to market changes, all while living in the same property.

- **Nomad™ with House Hacking** - Highly active. You're moving annually, setting up new living arrangements, and managing multiple properties as you go.
- **House Hacking with Traditional Buy and Hold** - Moderately active. You're managing long-term tenants while building a portfolio of properties.
- **House Hacking with Short-Term Rentals** - Extremely active. You're dealing with constant guest turnover, cleaning, and marketing, all while sharing your living space.

Scalability

Some investing strategies are more scalable than others.

Some variations of house hacking are more scalable than others.

Let's look at each variation to see how it might scale.

- **Traditional House Hacking** - Moderately scalable. You're typically limited to one property per year, assuming you're living in each property for at least a year. However, it requires only 5% down payment compared to 20% for traditional Buy and Hold, making it financially easier to scale. And, house hacking roommate income helps with both saving down payments and qualifying for loans.
- **Nomad™ with House Hacking** - Like *Traditional House Hacking*, but with a planned approach to move annually.

While this strategy allows for consistent property acquisition, it's slower compared to other investment methods where you could buy more than one per year. You can increase your acquisition speed by:

- o Incorporating short-term rentals with a 10% down payment second home in parallel.
- o Adding a non-owner-occupant strategy like traditional buy and hold alongside your house hacks.

- **House Hacking with Traditional Buy and Hold** - This combination can accelerate your portfolio growth. You're leveraging the no or low down-payment of house hacking while building a separate portfolio of traditional rentals in parallel. It requires more capital but can lead to faster scaling.
- **House Hacking with Short-Term Rentals** - Potentially the most scalable in terms of cash flow, but comes with a higher workload. The increased income can make it easier to qualify for loans on future properties making it easier to scale. The higher workload does slightly limit scaling. Consider building a team to manage the day-to-day operations as you scale to overcome workload constraints.

Risk Exposure

House hacking is considered a medium-risk strategy.

Here's why:

- **Amplified Returns** - Small down payments can lead to both higher gains and losses. Your returns get amplified more as you put down less.
- **Increased Likelihood of Negative Cash Flow** - Smaller down payments might result in your expenses exceeding your rental income. Negative cash flow is really just deferred down payment. If you had put more down, you wouldn't have negative cash flow. By putting less down, you're opting to pay negative cash flow (deferred down payment).
- **Price Decline During Ownership** - Market conditions or neighborhood changes could decrease your property's value.
- **Rent Decline During ownership** - Economic downturns might lead to lower rental rates, affecting your cash flow.
- **Credit Risk** - Failing to make mortgage payments could negatively impact your credit score.
- **Tenant/Property Management Risks** - Since you're renting the property you get all the typical tenant and property management risks associated with rentals.

House Hacking with Short-Term Rentals adds some additional risks.

Be prepared for:

- Changing local regulations that could impact your ability to operate.
- Potential HOA restrictions on short-term rentals.
- Higher insurance costs.

- More frequent turnover and increased wear and tear on your property.

The increased income from short-term rentals often balances out these additional risks.

Profit Speed

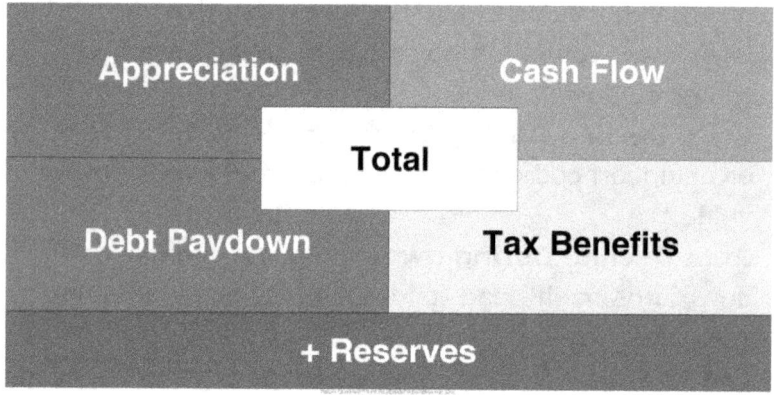

When it comes to house hacking, you're looking at four primary areas of return:

- **Appreciation** - The tendency for property values to increase over time.
- **Cash Flow** - The rental income you receive after expenses. This may show up as reduced—or completely eliminated—living costs while you're actively house hacking the property.
- **Debt Paydown** - Your tenants (or roommates) essentially help pay down your mortgage.
- **Tax Benefits** - Real estate offers various tax advantages, like depreciation.

There's also an additional return from reserves, which is the interest you earn on the money you've set aside to help handle emergencies on the property.

How quickly do you make money with house hacking? You typically see profit immediately.

Here's why:

- Reduced living expenses kick in as soon as you move in with roommates.
- Rents and security deposits are usually paid in advance.
- If you're using a lease-option strategy, you might also see an upfront option fee.

There are some cases where payments might be delayed slightly:

- **Short-Term Rentals** - If you're doing short-term rentals while living in the property, you might see a slight delay waiting for payouts from the short-term rental platforms.
- **Property Manager** - If you're utilizing a property manager you might see a delay in receiving your payout from them for rents they've collected.

Remember, you're also building wealth through appreciation and debt paydown. While these benefits might not be immediately apparent in your bank account, they're steadily increasing your net worth over time.

These can be tapped if you choose to sell or refinance your rental property. Check out *Should I Sell My Rental Property?* and separately *Should I Refinance My Rental Property?* in

The Real Estate Investing Mentor series for more information on the calculations and considerations for selling or refinancing rental properties including different spreadsheets for each.

Finding House Hacking Deals

Finding the right properties is important for successful house hacking.

Here are the most common methods you'll likely use to find house hack properties:

Most Common Methods

- **Multiple Listing Service (MLS)** - The MLS typically provides you with the largest selection of properties to choose from. This comprehensive database offers a wide variety of suitable properties, from duplexes to single-family homes with basement apartments.
- **For Sale By Owner (FSBO)** - Properties listed without a real estate agent or broker. Two types:

  o **Actively Marketed** - Owners selling directly, often advertised online or with yard signs.
  o **Hidden** - Properties where owners aren't actively selling but might if approached. Requires marketing, networking, and/or connections in your target area.

More Unusual Method

- **Wholesalers** - Middlemen who find and pass on deals to investors. Wholesalers could be a great source of off-market properties, with some specializing in multi-family properties ideal for house hacking.

Searching for House Hacking Deals in the MLS

When searching for house hacking deals in the Multiple Listing Service (MLS), you may want to use specific search terms to uncover more likely house hack candidates.

Here are some tips to help you find the perfect property:

- **Multi-Family Properties** - Start by searching for "Duplex," "Triplex," and "Fourplex." These properties are designed for multiple units, making them ideal for house hacking. There may be an option for these types of properties and/or you may decide to search for these words to catch properties mis-entered by real estate agents.
- **In-Law Suites** - Look for and/or search for terms like "Mother-In-Law," "In-Law," or "Suite." These often indicate separate living spaces within a single-family home.
- **Separate Entrances** - Properties with "Separate Entrance" listings can offer privacy for you and your tenants, a key feature for successful house hacking.

- **Multiple Kitchens** - Having more than one kitchen can make it easier to create separate living spaces. Search for homes with more than one kitchen. For example, search for the word "kitchens" (plural) in the property description.
- **Accessory Dwelling Units (ADUs)** - Use terms like "ADU," "Accessory Dwelling Unit," or "Multi-Generation(al)" to find properties with additional living spaces.
- **Converted Spaces** - Look for "Basement Apartment," "Garage Apartment," "Cottage," "Compound," "Pool House," or "Boat House." These can be excellent options for creating rental units.
- **Wet Bars** - Properties with wet bars can often be easily converted into small kitchenettes, perfect for creating separate living areas.
- **RV Hookups** - Homes with RV hookups might have potential for adding a tiny home or mobile unit for additional rental income.
- **Short-Term Rental Potential** - Search for "Airbnb," "VRBO," "Vacation Rental," "Short-Term-Rental," or "STR" to find properties already set up for or suitable for short-term rentals.
- **Existing House Hacks** - Some listings might explicitly mention "House Hack" or "Roommate," indicating they're already set up for this strategy.
- **Non-Conforming Units** - Look for "Non-Conforming" properties. While you shouldn't violate local regulations, these could be ideal for roommate situations.

Analyzing Deals

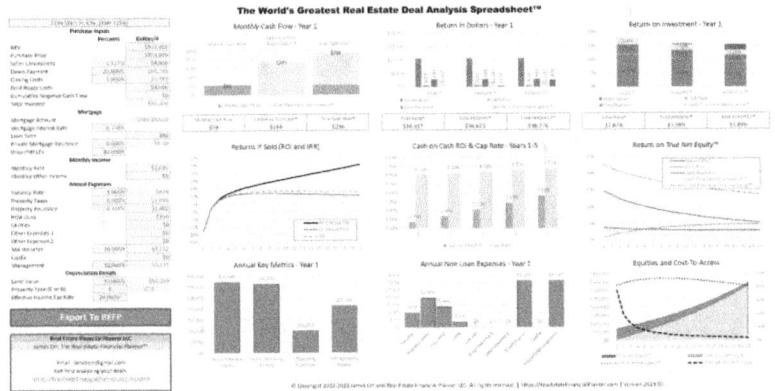

The World's Greatest Real Estate Deal Analysis Spreadsheet™

When it comes to analyzing house hacking deals, you need a reliable tool to crunch the numbers. That's where *The World's Greatest Real Estate Deal Analysis Spreadsheet™* comes in handy.

This spreadsheet was specifically designed to be able to handle house hacks in addition to the other most common rental property strategies. It helps you quickly evaluate potential properties, calculate cash flow, and determine if a deal meets your investment criteria.

Here's what the spreadsheet can do for you:

- Calculate potential rental income including from different units or by the room.
- Estimate cash flow and return on investment.
- Compare different house hacking strategy variations.

Ready to supercharge your house hacking deal analysis? You can download *The World's Greatest Real Estate Deal Analysis Spreadsheet*™ for free at:

https://REFP.com/spreadsheet

Market Conditions

When it comes to house hacking, understanding market conditions is an important consideration.

Let's dive into what makes a market ideal or challenging for this strategy.

Ideal Market Conditions

You're looking for:

- **Markets with Good Cash Flow** - This means the rental income from your housemates or tenants comfortably covers a significant portion of your expenses, including mortgage payments, taxes, insurance, HOA dues, and maintenance.
- **Markets with Strong Appreciation and Rent Appreciation** - Your property value and potential rental income grow over time, increasing your wealth and reducing your living costs.

These conditions lead to the most profitable house hacking situations.

Challenging Market Conditions

On the flip side, challenging market conditions can make house hacking much more difficult.

Watch out for:

- **Markets with High Property Values and Low Rents** – Properties with poor price to rent ratios tend to lead to more negative cash flow, even with reasonable down payments.
- **Markets with No or Negative Appreciation and Rent Appreciation** - Your property value and potential rental income stagnate or decrease, limiting your long-term gains and potentially increasing your living costs over time.

Remember, real estate markets are dynamic. A challenging market today might become ideal tomorrow, or vice versa.

Accessibility/Availability

The availability of house hacking deals can vary significantly depending on your market.

In many areas, you'll find plenty of options right on the Multiple Listing Service (MLS) and you'll be sifting and sorting to find the best options of many options available.

However, some markets might require more patience and strategy to find a property that will work as a house hack.

In particularly hot markets, finding properties with positive cash flow can be challenging, especially if you're working with a smaller down payment. You might need to utilize some creative financing strategies, apply some of the tools we have for improving cash flow or be prepared for some negative cash flow initially by setting aside the cumulative negative cash flow.

Keep in mind that interest rates play a huge role in whether a property will cash flow or not. A slight change in rates can make or break a deal. As an owner-occupant, you might qualify for better rates than traditional buy and hold investors.

Let's look at how availability might differ for various house hacking strategies:

- **Traditional House Hacking** - Generally the most available option. You'll find plenty of single-family homes and small multi-family properties on the MLS that could work for this strategy.
- **Student Rentals** - House hacking with students. Usually when you're a student and have other students as roommates. Availability may be limited to areas near colleges or universities.
- **Nomad™ with House Hacking** - Availability can vary. You'll need to find properties that work both as your primary residence and as future rentals.
- **House Hacking with Traditional Buy and Hold** - You'll need to find both house hacking properties and, separately, traditional buy and hold options.

- **House Hacking with Short-Term Rentals** - Availability varies widely depending on location. Popular tourist destinations may have more options but also more competition.

Using Retirement Account

When it comes to house hacking, using retirement accounts is much more difficult.

Unlike traditional buy and hold investing as a non-owner-occupant, house hacking involves living in the property you're investing in.

That's potentially problematic for directly utilizing self-directed retirement accounts to invest.

You can utilize traditional non-owner-occupant buy and hold strategies with self-directed retirement accounts like Self-Directed IRAs (SDIRAs) or Self-Directed 401(k)s (SD401Ks).

But self-directed retirement accounts typically can't be used for properties you're going to occupy. This means they're off-limits for most house hacking strategies.

The IRS has strict rules about using retirement funds for personal benefit before retirement age. Living in a property purchased with these funds is seen as a prohibited transaction.

However, you may want to do the math to see if paying the penalty to withdraw funds early from your retirement accounts (self-directed or otherwise) makes sense. In some cases, the returns you earn by house hacking might be compelling enough that paying a penalty is worthwhile.

Or, consider partnering with someone else who has a self-directed retirement account and utilize that to invest in your house hacks.

BONUS CHAPTERS

Introduction to Real Estate Deal Analysis

Analyzing real estate deals can be a daunting task, but with the right tools and knowledge, it becomes much more manageable. One powerful tool we recommend is *The World's Greatest Real Estate Deal Analysis Spreadsheet*™. This spreadsheet is designed to help you evaluate the financial viability of real estate investments with ease and precision.

In our book, *How to Analyze Real Estate Deals*, we delve deep into the intricacies of deal analysis, providing step-by-step instructions and expert insights. This introduction aims to give you a high-level overview of the process and how to effectively use the spreadsheet to make informed investment decisions.

The spreadsheet allows you to input various data points such as purchase price, mortgage details, monthly income, and annual expenses. It then performs complex calculations to provide you with key metrics like cash flow, return on investment (ROI), and internal rate of return (IRR).

By leveraging this tool, you can:

- Quickly assess the profitability of potential deals.
- Compare multiple investment opportunities.
- Make data-driven decisions to maximize your returns.

Whether you're a seasoned investor or just starting out, understanding how to analyze real estate deals is crucial for success.

Download Spreadsheet for Free

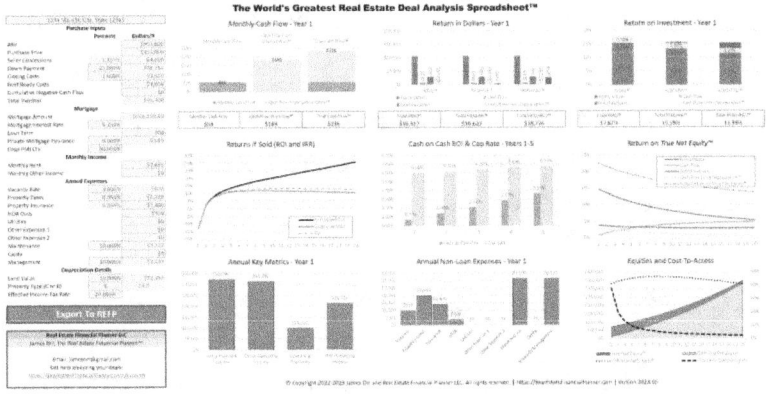

Unlock the full potential of your real estate investments by downloading *The World's Greatest Real Estate Deal Analysis Spreadsheet*™ for free.

Get your copy at: https://REFP.info/spreadsheet

We recommend always keeping an unedited, fresh copy on your hard drive in case you can't download the spreadsheet in the future.

Before analyzing a property, always make a new copy.

Spreadsheet Inputs

Entering the inputs into the spreadsheet is simple. Here's what you need to know:

- The manila fields indicate where you should input your data.
- The gray background with blue text shows the calculations that are automatically performed for you.

First, please name the deal that you're analyzing in the field just above the "Purchase Inputs". This will allow you to know which deal you're looking at if you're considering analyzing multiple deals or one deal multiple ways.

Purchase Inputs

Before we dive into the specifics of analyzing a real estate deal, let's go over the inputs required for the spreadsheet. These inputs will be divided into two columns: one for percentages and one for dollar amounts (or numbers).

Understanding what to enter in each field is crucial for accurately analyzing your deal. Let's go over what to put in each field next.

- **ARV** - Enter the After Repair Value, which is the estimated value of the property after all repairs and improvements have been made.
- **Purchase Price** - Enter the amount you are paying to acquire the property from the seller.
- **Seller Concessions** - Enter any financial concessions or incentives that the seller has agreed to provide, such as covering closing costs or offering repair credits.
- **Down Payment** - Enter the initial amount you will pay out-of-pocket towards the purchase of the property. Be sure to check out our guide on creative ways to come up with down payments for rental properties.
- **Closing Costs** - Enter the total costs associated with closing the real estate transaction, including title insurance, attorney fees, and other related expenses.
- **Rent Ready Costs** - Enter the expenses required to make the property ready for tenants, such as cleaning, repairs, and any necessary upgrades.
- **Cumulative Negative Cash Flow** - If you have negative cash flow enter the total cumulative amount of negative cash flow you anticipate before the property becomes cash flow positive. We recommend you set this aside to reduce risk. You may also want to check out our book on *How to Improve Cash Flow on Rental Properties* to get rid of negative cash flow on your properties.
- **Total Invested** - This is calculated for you. It is the cumulative amount of money you have invested in the

property, including **Down Payment, Closing Costs, Rent Ready Costs, Cumulative Negative Cash Flow**, minus any **Seller Concessions** you received from the seller.

Mortgage Inputs

To accurately analyze your real estate deal, it's essential to input detailed information about your mortgage and financing. These inputs will help calculate your monthly payments, interest costs, and overall financial commitment. Here's what you'll need to enter:

- **Mortgage Amount** - This is calculated for you. It is the total amount of money you are borrowing to finance the purchase of the property.
- **Mortgage Interest Rate** - Enter the annual interest rate for your mortgage. This is the percentage of the loan amount that you will pay as interest each year.
- **Loan Term** - Enter the duration of your mortgage loan in months. 360 months is a 30-year loan. This is the period over which you will repay the loan.
- **Private Mortgage Insurance** - Enter the monthly cost of private mortgage insurance (PMI) if applicable. PMI is typically required if your down payment is less than 20% of the purchase price. If you don't have PMI, use 0.000% here.
- **Drop PMI LTV** - Enter the loan-to-value (LTV) ratio at which PMI will be dropped. This is the point at which your equity in the property is high enough that PMI is no

longer required. If you don't have PMI, use 0.000% here.

Monthly Income

Accurately estimating your monthly income is critical for assessing the profitability of your real estate investment. This section will guide you through the necessary inputs for calculating your expected monthly income from the property, including rent and any additional sources of income.

- **Monthly Rent** - Enter the amount of rent you expect to receive from tenants each month. If you don't know how to determine what rent is on a property you're considering, you might want to check out our book on *How to Determine Rent Comps*.
- **Monthly Other Income** - Enter any additional monthly income from the property, such as parking fees, laundry services, or storage rentals.

Annual Expenses

Understanding and accurately estimating annual expenses is crucial for analyzing the financial viability of a real estate investment. This section will guide you through the various costs associated with owning and maintaining a property, from vacancy rates to property taxes and insurance. By thoroughly accounting for each of these expenses, you can better predict your investment's profitability and make more informed decisions.

- **Vacancy Rate** - Enter the percentage of time the property is expected to be vacant each year.
- **Property Taxes** - Enter the annual property tax amount you will pay for owning the property.
- **Property Insurance** - Enter the annual cost of insuring the property.
- **HOA Dues** - Enter the annual homeowner association fees, if applicable.
- **Utilities** - Enter the annual cost of utilities that you will pay as the property owner.
- **Other Expenses 1 and 2** - Enter any other annual expenses not covered in the previous categories.
- **Maintenance** - Enter the annual cost of maintaining the property, including repairs and routine upkeep.
- **CapEx** - Enter the annual amount set aside for capital expenditures. Consider our book and spreadsheet on CapEx for more guidance.
- **Management** - Enter the annual cost of property management services, if applicable.

Depreciation Details

Depreciation is a critical aspect of real estate investment analysis, as it allows you to account for the gradual reduction in the value of your property over time. Properly calculating and understanding depreciation can provide significant tax benefits and improve the overall financial picture of your investment. This section will guide you through the necessary inputs for determining depreciation, including land value, property type, and your effective income tax rate. By accurately inputting these details, you can optimize your investment strategy and maximize potential returns.

- **Land Value** - Enter the percent of the property that represents the value of the land. This value is used to calculate depreciation.
- **Property Type (C or R)** - Indicate whether the property is classified as commercial (C) or residential (R). This affects the depreciation schedule.
- **Effective Income Tax Rate** - Enter your effective income tax rate. This rate is used to estimate the tax benefits of depreciation.

Overrides

The spreadsheet is designed to be user-friendly on the Dashboard, while offering extensive functionality in the Overrides section. This dual approach ensures that users can easily navigate and input basic data, but also have access to more advanced features when needed.

In the Overrides tab, you have the ability to:

- **Modify any other inputs** - Adjust various parameters to suit your specific needs and scenarios.
- **Perform custom calculations** - Create and implement your own unique calculations to gain deeper insights into your investments.

- **View intermediate calculations** - Access detailed breakdowns of the calculations that drive the final results, providing transparency and better understanding.
- **Analyze performance over an extended period** - The spreadsheet allows you to conduct analysis through up to 40 years, enabling long-term strategic planning.
- **Track investment performance** - Use the Overrides tab to monitor how your investment evolves over time, making it easier to adjust your strategy as needed.

This comprehensive functionality ensures that the spreadsheet is not only a powerful tool for initial analysis but also a valuable resource for ongoing management and optimization of your real estate investments.

Dashboard

The Dashboard section provides a comprehensive overview of your real estate investment's key metrics and financial performance.

Here, you can quickly assess your monthly cash flow, return on investment (ROI), internal rate of return (IRR), and other critical indicators.

The Dashboard is designed to offer a user-friendly summary of your investment, allowing you to make informed decisions and track your progress over time.

Of course, you can dig into the Overrides tab for a ridiculous amount of additional detail.

Monthly Cash Flow - Year 1

This chart displays the Monthly Cash Flow, *Cash Flow from Depreciation*™, and the combined total, referred to as *True Cash Flow*™.

Understanding these metrics is crucial as they provide a comprehensive view of your investment's financial health.

- Monthly Cash Flow shows the actual cash inflow and outflow.
- *Cash Flow from Depreciation*™ accounts for tax benefits derived from property depreciation.
- *True Cash Flow*™ combines these figures, offering a more accurate representation of your investment's profitability.

Return in Dollars - Year 1

This chart displays the estimated dollars earned from your real estate investment over the first year, including Appreciation, Cash Flow, *Cash Flow from Depreciation*™, and Debt Paydown.

Understanding these metrics provides a holistic view of your investment's performance:

- **Appreciation** - Reflects the increase in property value over the year.
- **Cash Flow** - Shows the actual cash inflow and outflow.
- ***Cash Flow from Depreciation*™** - Accounts for tax benefits derived from property depreciation.

- **Debt Paydown** - Indicates the amount of principal paid down on your mortgage over the year.

Additionally, the chart includes earnings on reserves:

- **6 Months of Reserves in Savings** - Illustrates the interest earned if you set aside 6 months of reserves in a savings account.
- **Most of 12 Months of Reserves in Another Investment** - Shows the potential earnings if most of 12 months of reserves are invested in another investment vehicle like the stock market.

These combined figures provide a comprehensive representation of your investment's profitability and financial health over the first year.

You can see the totals at the bottom of the chart.

Return on Investment - Year 1

This chart displays the return on investment (ROI) from your real estate investment over the first year, including Appreciation, Cash Flow, *Cash Flow from Depreciation*™, and Debt Paydown.

Understanding these metrics provides a holistic view of your investment's performance:

- **Appreciation** - Reflects the increase in property value over the year divided by the total amount invested (and reserves where applicable).

- **Cash Flow** - Shows the actual cash inflow and outflow divided by the total amount invested (and reserves where applicable).
- *Cash Flow from Depreciation*™ - Accounts for tax benefits derived from property depreciation divided by the total amount invested (and reserves where applicable).
- **Debt Paydown** - Indicates the amount of principal paid down on your mortgage over the year divided by the total amount invested (and reserves where applicable).

Additionally, the chart includes ROI on reserves:

- **6 Months of Reserves in Savings** - Illustrates the interest earned if you set aside 6 months of reserves in a savings account, divided by the total amount invested plus 6 months of reserves.
- **Most of 12 Months of Reserves in Another Investment** - Shows the potential earnings if most of 12 months of reserves are invested in another investment vehicle like the stock market, divided by the total amount invested plus 12 months of reserves.

These combined figures provide a comprehensive representation of your investment's profitability and financial health over the first year in terms of ROI.

You can see the totals at the bottom of the chart.

48

Returns if Sold (ROI and IRR)

This chart illustrates the return on investment if you sold the property each year for the first 20 years. It includes three key metrics:

- **Simple Annualized Return on Investment** - This metric shows the average annual return on your investment, calculated by dividing the total return by the number of years you held the property.
- **Compound Annualized Return on Investment** - This metric accounts for the compounding effect, showing the average annual return on your investment when considering the reinvestment of earnings.
- **Internal Rate of Return (IRR)** - This metric represents the annualized rate of return that makes the net present value (NPV) of all cash flows (both inflows and outflows) from the investment equal to zero.

These metrics provide a comprehensive view of the financial performance of your investment over time, helping you to understand the potential long-term profitability and compare it with other investment opportunities.

Cash on Cash ROI & Cap Rate - Years 1-5

This chart displays the Cash on Cash Return on Investment (ROI) and the Capitalization Rate (Cap Rate) for the property over the first 5 years.

Understanding these metrics provides a comprehensive view of your investment's performance:

- **Cash on Cash ROI** - This metric shows the annual return on your investment based on the actual cash invested. It is calculated by dividing the annual pre-tax cash flow by the total cash invested.
- **Cap Rate** - This metric represents the annual return on the property based on its current market value. It is calculated by dividing the net operating income (NOI) by the property's current market value.

By understanding these metrics, you can gauge the effectiveness and profitability of your investment, enabling you to make well-informed decisions and evaluate it against other potential investment opportunities.

Return on True Net Equity™

This chart shows you the returns you're earning from Appreciation, Cash Flow, *Cash Flow from Depreciation*™, and Debt Paydown divided by the equity minus the costs to access that equity with a sale (what we call True Net Equity™). It shows the first 20 years. It also shows the total of all four areas of return.

Understanding these metrics is crucial for assessing the true profitability of your real estate investment:

- **Appreciation** - Reflects the increase in property value over the year.
- **Cash Flow** - Shows the actual cash inflow and outflow.

- *Cash Flow from Depreciation*™ - Accounts for tax benefits derived from property depreciation.
- **Debt Paydown** - Indicates the amount of principal paid down on your mortgage over the year.

By dividing these returns by the True Net Equity™, you get a more accurate representation of your investment's performance, considering the costs to access the equity. This comprehensive view helps in making informed decisions and comparing the potential returns of different investments.

For more information on True Net Equity™ consider checking out our books about that:

- Should I Sell My Rental My Rental Property?
- Should I Sell My Refinance My Rental Property?

Annual Key Metrics - Year 1

This chart displays the financial performance of your real estate investment in terms of Gross Potential Income (GPI), Gross Operating Income (GOI), Operating Expenses (OpEx), and Net Operating Income (NOI) for the first year.

Understanding these metrics provides a comprehensive view of your investment's revenue and profitability:

- **Gross Potential Income (GPI)** - This metric represents the total income the property could generate if it were fully rented and all units were occupied at market rent rates, without accounting for any vacancies or losses.

- **Gross Operating Income (GOI)** - This metric reflects the actual income received from the property, including rent and other income sources, after accounting for vacancies and any collection losses.
- **Operating Expenses (OpEx)** - These are the costs associated with maintaining and managing the property, excluding mortgage payments and capital expenditures.
- **Net Operating Income (NOI)** - This metric is calculated by subtracting the operating expenses from the Gross Operating Income. It represents the income generated by the property after all operating expenses have been deducted.

By understanding these metrics, you can better assess the financial health and profitability of your real estate investment, helping you make more strategic decisions and compare it with other investment opportunities.

Annual Non-Loan Expenses - Year 1

This chart displays the financial performance of your real estate investment by itemizing all the non-loan expenses for the first year. Understanding these metrics provides a comprehensive view of your property's operational costs, which are crucial for accurate financial analysis and planning:

- **Vacancy Rate** - The percentage of time the property is expected to be vacant each year.
- **Property Taxes** - The annual amount paid for property taxes.

- **Property Insurance** - The cost of insuring the property for the year.
- **HOA Dues** - Annual homeowner association fees, if applicable.
- **Utilities** - The total annual cost of utilities paid by the property owner.
- **Other Expenses 1 and 2** - Any additional annual expenses not covered in the previous categories.
- **Maintenance** - The annual expense for maintaining the property, including routine repairs and upkeep.
- **CapEx** - The annual amount set aside for capital expenditures, such as major repairs or replacements.
- **Management Fees** - The cost of property management services, if utilized.

By breaking down these non-loan expenses, this chart helps you understand the total operational costs associated with your property, enabling you to better manage your investment and forecast its financial performance.

Equities and Cost-To-Access

This chart displays the equity in your real estate deal each year for the first 20 years, focusing on two key metrics: *True Net Equity*™ and Cash-Out Refi Equity.

- *True Net Equity*™ - This is the equity minus the costs to access it through a sale. It shows the real profit after considering selling costs.

- **Cash-Out Refi Equity** - This is the equity available if you refinance the property. It helps you understand the potential funds available through refinancing.
- **Cost-To-Access Equity Percentages** - The chart also shows the costs (as a percentage of the equity) associated with accessing each type of equity. This provides insight into the expenses involved.

Understanding these metrics is crucial for knowing how much money you could pull out of the investment over time and the cost to access that equity if you choose to do so.

Trademarks: The World's Greatest Real Estate Deal Analysis Spreadsheet™, Cash Flow from Depreciation™, True Cash Flow, True Net Equity™, and Nomad™ are trademarks of James Orr and/or Real Estate Financial Planner LLC. All rights reserved.

94 Ways to Improve Cash Flow on Rental Properties

You might find yourself in a real estate market where:

- Property prices are high—possibly even soaring,
- Mortgage interest rates are elevated—maybe significantly so,
- Yet rents, despite any increases, haven't risen enough to offset these higher prices and rates.

Instead of the steady stream of cash flow you anticipated, you may be seeing just a trickle.

As a real estate broker, I developed the *Lowest Monthly Payment Guarantee*™ for my clients. This comprehensive checklist—backed by a *cash-in-your-pocket guarantee*—promised to uncover every possible way to reduce and minimize their monthly payments when purchasing a property.

For my real estate investor clients, I went a step further and created the *Maximum Cash Flow Guarantee*™. This second checklist—also backed by a *cash-in-your-pocket guarantee*—was designed to help them identify every possible way to increase and maximize the income generated from their rental properties.

Simply put, cash flow is the difference between income and expenses.

By maximizing income and minimizing expenses on a rental property, you can significantly boost your cash flow.

Below, you'll find an abridged version of these two checklists—combined into one—designed to help you maximize cash flow on your rental properties.

For your convenience, I've organized the strategies into seven distinct stages of the real estate investing process.

7 Distinct Real Estate Investing Stages for Improving Cash Flow

The real estate investing process can be broken down into seven distinct stages, each offering unique opportunities to improve cash flow:

1. **Searching for Properties** - Strategies to enhance cash flow while you're searching for a property to buy.

2. **Financing the Property** - Tactics to maximize cash flow when securing financing for the property you're purchasing.

3. **Improving the Real Estate Investing Strategy** - Different real estate investing strategies produce varying levels of cash flow. Here, you'll find strategies tailored to the specific investing approach you choose once you've acquired the property.

4. **Improving the Property** - Cash flow enhancement strategies based on making physical improvements to the property itself.

5. **Marketing the Property for Rent** - Techniques to boost cash flow during the process of marketing your property to prospective tenants.

6. **While Owning the Property** - Strategies you can implement at any time during ownership to optimize cash flow.

7. **While Renting the Property** - Methods to improve cash flow while actively renting out the property.

While applying strategies from each stage will maximize your cash flow, you can also focus on the stage you're currently in. Implement what you can now, and revisit these strategies regularly to continuously improve—aim for just a 1% improvement each month.

Searching for Properties

Here are the cash flow improving strategies to implement while searching for a property to buy.

- **Agent Selection** - Choosing the right real estate agent can have a significant impact on your investment's cash flow. Some agents offer lower commissions or commission rebates. This money can appear as improved cash flow in the first year or use the money to buy down your mortgage interest rate and get improved cash flow for the life of the loan.

- **Lock/Float** - When securing financing for a property, interest rates can fluctuate. Locking in an interest rate early can protect you from rising rates during the closing process, while floating allows you to benefit from potential rate drops. This decision can directly influence your cash flow by affecting your monthly mortgage payments. This is especially important when buying properties that have extended under contract periods like when buying new construction.

- **Search for Less Expensive Properties** - Lower-priced properties often come with smaller mortgage payments, which can improve cash flow if you're able to get the same rent as their more expensive alternatives. For every $10,000 less expensive the property, you save approximately $50 per month (when mortgage rates are in the 5% range). Some lower priced prices will have commensurately lower rents. Analyze each deal carefully to ensure that the overall income and expenses align to boost your cash flow.

- **Search for Pretty Properties** - Consider purchasing properties that are already in good condition and don't require significant fix-up costs. By doing so, you can allocate funds that would have been used for repairs to increase your down payment or buy down the interest rate, both of which can lead to better cash flow.

- **Search for Seller Concessions** - Seller concessions are contributions from the seller to help cover your closing costs. By negotiating for these concessions, you can reduce your out-of-pocket expenses or even use them to buy down your mortgage interest rate, both of which enhance cash flow. Consider searching for properties that are offering seller concessions.
- **Search for Creative Financing** - Creative financing can offer more favorable terms than traditional loans, directly impacting your cash flow. Here are several types of creative financing to consider:

  - **Search for Owner Financing** - Owner financing involves the seller acting as the lender, which can lead to better terms than a traditional bank loan. This can reduce your monthly payments and improve cash flow. We define owner financing as when the seller does not have a mortgage; if they have a mortgage that's wrap financing or buying the property subject to their existing mortgage which we will cover next.
  - **Search for Wrap Financing** - In wrap financing, you agree to pay the seller a monthly amount that "wraps" around their existing mortgage. The seller keeps their original mortgage in place and continues making payments to their lender. You, in turn, make payments to the seller that cover both the existing mortgage and any additional amount you've agreed upon. This can result in a lower overall interest rate compared to obtaining new financing, which can

improve your cash flow. Wrap financing also gives the seller the protection of foreclosure rights if you fail to make payments.

- o **Search for Subject To**- In a "subject to" arrangement, you take ownership of the property while the seller's original mortgage stays in place. Instead of wrapping a new loan around the old one, you take over making payments directly to the lender on the seller's existing loan. The loan remains in the seller's name, but you're responsible for the payments. You're not formally accountable to the lender—it's not on your credit report—but you are responsible to the seller as per your agreement. This can be advantageous if the seller's mortgage has a lower interest rate than what's currently available. Like wrap financing, this can significantly reduce your mortgage expenses and boost cash flow. However, "subject to" financing typically doesn't offer the seller the same foreclosure protections as wrap financing does.

- o **Search for Assumable Loans** - Some loans can be formally transferred from the seller to the buyer, keeping the original interest rate intact. If the seller's loan has a lower interest rate, assuming the loan can significantly boost your cash flow. Since most loan assumptions are for owner-occupant borrowers this strategy likely only applies to those utilizing an owner-occupant investing strategy like house hacking or Nomad™.

- o **Search for Rent-To-Own Properties** - Rent-to-own agreements allow you to lease a property with the

60

option to purchase it later. These arrangements can offer lower initial payments and more flexible terms, which may improve your cash flow compared to traditional financing.

- o **Search for Agreements for Deed** - Also called bond for deed, contract for deed, or installment land contracts, these arrangements let you pay the seller directly over time. You get the deed after fulfilling the contract. This can lead to lower payments and improved cash flow while you're repaying.
- o **Search for Seller Financing** - Seller financing typically involves the seller offering a loan to cover a portion of the purchase price, often as a second mortgage or "carryback" loan. In this scenario, you would secure the primary mortgage from a traditional lender, and the seller finances the remaining balance. For example, if you purchase a property for $200,000, you might get a $160,000 loan from a bank, with the seller providing a $40,000 loan. This setup can result in more favorable terms, such as lower interest rates or flexible payment schedules, improving your overall cash flow. Unlike owner financing, where the seller finances the entire purchase, seller financing usually complements other financing sources, reducing the need for a larger bank loan.

Once you've found a promising property using the strategies above, the next step is to optimize your financing to further enhance your cash flow. Let's explore the various ways you can improve your cash flow during the financing stage of your real estate investment.

Financing the Property

Here are the cash flow improving strategies to implement while financing the property you're buying.

Before Getting Loan

Here are a few strategies to improve cash flow to use before getting your loan.

- **Lender Selection** - Shop around for lenders to find one that offers better interest rates, lower fees, or more favorable terms. Different lenders have varying costs and requirements, so comparing multiple options on the same day can ensure you get the best deal, improving your overall cash flow.
- **Select by Closing Costs** - Some loans come with higher closing costs than others. By selecting a loan with lower closing costs, especially if you plan to finance these costs, you can reduce the amount you need to borrow, leading to better cash flow due to lower monthly payments.
- **Lock/Float** - Decide whether to lock in your interest rate early to protect against potential rate increases before closing, or to float and take advantage of possible rate decreases. Locking your rate provides security, while floating offers flexibility, both of which can impact your cash flow depending on market conditions.

- **Offer Less** - Negotiating a lower purchase price directly reduces the amount you need to finance, leading to lower monthly mortgage payments. This strategy can also leave more of your resources available for other cash flow improvement tactics.

Pay Upfront Instead of Financing

Here are some strategies for improving cash flow that deal with opting to pay fees upfront instead of financing them.

- **Seller Concessions** - Negotiate for the seller to cover some of your closing costs or to provide credits that can be used to buy down your mortgage interest rate. This is almost certainly required to be done at the time you make your offer and not after your offer is accepted. This reduces your upfront cash outlay and can lower your monthly mortgage payments, thereby improving cash flow.
- **Pay Closing Costs** - Paying your closing costs upfront instead of rolling them into your mortgage can reduce the amount you borrow, lowering your monthly payments and improving cash flow over the life of the loan.
- **Pre-Pay PMI** - If you're required to pay Private Mortgage Insurance (PMI), consider pre-paying it in a lump sum rather than monthly. This reduces your ongoing monthly expenses, leading to better cash flow.
- **Staggered Rate** - Opt for a staggered interest rate loan, where the interest rate is lower in the initial years

and increases over time. This can provide you with better cash flow during the early years of the loan when you may need it most.

- **Buy Down Rate** - Pay upfront to lower your mortgage interest rate for the life of the loan. A lower interest rate means a lower monthly payment, which can significantly improve your cash flow over time. For long-term buy and hold real estate investors—especially if you find yourself in a low mortgage interest rate environment—this can be an amazing strategy.

Change/Improve Borrower(s)

These strategies for improving cash flow relate to changing or improving the borrower on the loan.

- **Credit Score** - Improving your credit score can help you secure a lower interest rate and reduce your PMI rate. Both of these improvements lead to lower monthly payments and better cash flow.
- **Add Borrower** - Adding a co-borrower with a strong credit profile to your loan can help you qualify for a better interest rate and lower PMI, both of which can enhance your cash flow.
- **Remove Borrower** - If one borrower has a weaker credit profile, removing them from the loan might result in a better interest rate. This can lead to lower monthly payments and improved cash flow.
- **Loan Partner** - Partnering with someone who has a strong financial profile can help you secure better loan

terms, including lower interest rates and more favorable conditions, which ultimately enhance your cash flow.

Relationship With Lender

These cash flow improving strategies are based on your relationship with the lender or lending institution.

- **Auto Pay Loan** - Setting up automatic payments can sometimes qualify you for a slight reduction in your interest rate, directly improving your cash flow by lowering your monthly mortgage payment. It may show up also as a penalty to the interest rate if you don't use autopay for the mortgage.
- **Additional Accounts** - Maintaining additional accounts or depositing more funds with your lender might earn you a small interest rate reduction, leading to improved cash flow through lower monthly payments. This is more common with commercial loans and relationship banking.

Change Amortization

These strategies to improve your cash flow deal with changing the amortization schedule of the financing you're getting.

- **Interest Only** - An interest-only loan allows you to pay only the interest for a certain period, which significantly reduces your monthly payments. This can boost your cash flow in the short term, though it comes with long-term risks since the principal remains unpaid. You'll need to have a solid plan to deal with the loan balance when the ballon payment date arrives.

- **Negative Amortization** - A negative amortizing loan allows you to pay less than the interest due, causing the loan balance to increase over time. This lowers your initial payments and improves short-term cash flow but increases your debt over time.
- **Rate from Loan Term** - Shortening the loan term (e.g., switching from a 30-year to a 15-year mortgage) can lower your interest rate. However, this typically increases your monthly payments, so it's more about long-term savings than immediate cash flow improvement.
- **Loan Term** - Extending the loan term (e.g., from 30 to 40 years) reduces the monthly payment amount, which can improve your cash flow. However, this means you'll pay more interest over the life of the loan.

Loan Terms

These cash flow improving strategies deal with the terms (details) of the loan itself.

- **Amount Borrowed** - Putting more money down reduces the amount you need to borrow, leading to lower monthly payments. This can improve your cash flow, though it also means tying up more capital in the property.

- **Loan-To-Value** - A lower loan-to-value (LTV) ratio, achieved by making a larger down payment, often results in a better interest rate. This lowers your monthly payments and improves cash flow. Not only can putting more down improve your LTV and give you a better interest rate, but it might also reduce your Private Mortgage Insurance (PMI) payment since that's part of the calculation for determining PMI amounts.
- **Adjustable Rate** - An adjustable-rate mortgage (ARM) typically starts with a lower interest rate than a fixed-rate mortgage. This can enhance your cash flow in the initial years, though the rate—and your payments—can increase later.

Private Mortgage Insurance (PMI)

These strategies to improve cash flow deal primarily with Private Mortgage Insurance (PMI).

What is PMI? The lender would prefer you put at least 20% down to finance a property. With 20% down they feel comfortable enough that if you don't pay as agreed they will be able to foreclose, sell the property and get all their money back after the expenses of foreclosure and sale.

You insist on putting less than 20% down.

They may reluctantly agree, but they may charge you a higher interest rate because it is a riskier loan to them. And, additionally, they may insist that you pay a third-party insurance company a fee that insures them in case you default and they're unable to foreclose and sell the property to recoup their entire investment. This third-party insurance company is Private Mortgage Insurance.

It is insurance you pay for to protect the lender in case you default on the loan.

- **Eliminate PMI** - If you can put down at least 20% of the purchase price, you can avoid PMI altogether, significantly reducing your monthly mortgage expenses and improving your cash flow.
- **Pre-Pay PMI** - Paying PMI in a lump sum upfront instead of monthly can reduce your ongoing costs, leading to better cash flow throughout the loan term.
- **Improve Credit** - Enhancing your credit score can help you secure a lower PMI rate or even eliminate PMI altogether if your LTV ratio improves, both of which contribute to better cash flow.
- **Add Borrowers** - Added a borrower to your loan typically reduces PMI and therefore improves cash flow.

Other Properties

These cash flow improving strategies rely on tapping into other properties you own.

Some of these strategies deal with making sure your cash flow is optimized for your entire portfolio (including these other properties) and not specifically to a new property you're buying.

- **Cash Out Refi to Buy/Refi** - Consider doing a cash-out refinance on another property to use the proceeds for purchasing or refinancing your current property. This can result in better overall financing terms and improved cash flow.
- **Cash Out Refi for Larger Down Payment** - If putting more down on your current property will secure a better interest rate or eliminate PMI, consider using funds from a cash-out refinance on another property. This can lower your monthly payments and improve cash flow.
- **Rate and Term Before Acquisition** - Before purchasing a new property, consider refinancing your existing properties to better terms. As you own more properties the complexity of refinancing increases significantly. Consider this a reminder to consider this before each new purchase and to make any changes to other properties now before you add a new property that further limits what you can do. This can also improve the overall cash flow on your portfolio and might also allow you to qualify for better financing on the new purchase.

Non-Traditional Financing

These are some non-traditional financing strategies for improving cash flow you might want to consider.

- **Pay Cash** - If you have sufficient funds, paying cash for a property eliminates the need for financing altogether, which maximizes cash flow by removing monthly mortgage payments.

- **Private Financing** - Secure a loan from family or friends (private lenders) who might offer more favorable terms than traditional banks. This can lead to lower monthly payments and improved cash flow.
- **Creative Financing** - Explore options like owner financing, wrap financing, agreement for deed, lease-options, or subject to, where the seller might offer better terms than traditional lenders. These strategies can lower your mortgage payments and enhance cash flow.
- **Assumable Loan** - If the seller's existing loan has a lower interest rate than current market rates, assuming their loan can be a great way to secure better financing terms, leading to improved cash flow. This is more likely for owner-occupant loans, so this is probably limited to owner-occupant investing strategies like house hacking or Nomad™.

While optimizing your financing is crucial for improving cash flow, it's equally important to consider how your chosen real estate investing strategy can impact your returns. Let's now explore various strategies that can enhance your cash flow by refining your overall investment approach.

Improving the Real Estate Investing Strategy

Here are the cash flow improving strategies based on improving the real estate investing strategy you're opting to utilize.

- **Term** - Adjusting the duration of your lease can significantly impact your cash flow. Shorter-term rentals, such as daily, weekly, or monthly leases, often command higher rents compared to yearly leases. However, shorter terms can also lead to increased expenses, including higher vacancy rates, more frequent marketing, and potentially higher management and maintenance costs. Offering different terms, such as furnished vs. unfurnished rentals, can also cater to various market segments, like vacation rentals or boarding houses, providing opportunities to maximize income.

- **Lease-Option** - Lease-option strategies, including variations like rent-to-own (like lease-purchases and lease-options), can dramatically improve cash flow, particularly in markets where buying is significantly more expensive than renting. These arrangements typically involve collecting a non-refundable purchase deposit/option fee, which can—mathematically—appear to add hundreds of dollars per month to your cash flow. Additionally, tenants in lease-option agreements often treat the property with more care, reducing maintenance, vacancy, and management costs. This strategy is a form of our *Deal Alchemy*™, where you trade future appreciation returns for immediate cash flow.

- **Niche** - Specializing in a specific rental market can allow you to charge premium rents by catering to unique needs. For example, you might focus on corporate rentals, traveling nurses, or student housing. By understanding and addressing the specific requirements of your niche audience, such as providing furnished units for corporate rentals or flexible leases for students, you can add value that justifies higher rental rates. The key is to determine what additional services or amenities you can offer that will attract your target market and what premium you can reasonably charge for those services.

The following cash flow improving strategies are really just variations of house hacking where you're renting out part of the property you're living in for income and to improve cash flow. However, you could utilize these strategies even when you're not living in the property.

- **Roommates** - Renting out individual bedrooms in a single-family home, or additional units in a duplex, triplex, or fourplex, can significantly increase your cash flow. This is a common house hacking strategy where you live in one part of the property and rent out the rest. For example, you might rent out spare bedrooms in your own home or lease the other units in a multi-family property. This approach allows you to maximize the rental income from a single property by utilizing every available space.

- **Rent by Bed/Bedroom** - Some properties, particularly those near colleges or universities, may lend themselves well to renting by the bedroom or even by the bed. This strategy works particularly well with student housing, where multiple tenants share a single property. By renting out each bedroom or bed individually, you can often achieve a higher overall rent compared to leasing the entire property to a single tenant.

- **Rent by Parts** - Renting out different parts of a property, such as non-conforming units in a duplex, triplex, or fourplex, can be a lucrative strategy. It's essential to check local occupancy laws to ensure compliance. This strategy can also include more unconventional setups, such as renting out RV parking spaces, tiny homes, garages, or storage units on the property. These spaces don't have to be residential; they can be rented for commercial or recreational purposes, such as storage or use of shared community amenities like a pool or recreational center.

While optimizing your real estate investing strategy can significantly boost cash flow, another powerful approach is to enhance the property itself. By making strategic improvements and modifications to your rental property, you can potentially increase its value and appeal, leading to higher rental income and improved cash flow. Let's explore some effective strategies for improving cash flow through property enhancements.

Improving the Property

Here are the cash flow improving strategies based on making improvements to the property.

- **Subdivide** - Consider subdividing your property into multiple units to increase rental income. For example, you could rent the upstairs and downstairs separately, offering tenants more privacy while still sharing common areas like heating, cooling, mail, laundry, and possibly even the kitchen or living areas. This isn't the same as converting the property into a formal duplex or triplex; instead, it's more about creating a roommate-like situation with more separation. This setup allows you to comply with local roommate laws and zoning requirements while potentially charging higher rents, as tenants may feel like they have their own space.
- **Upgrade Property** - Enhancing your property's curb appeal and overall condition can justify charging higher rents. Improvements could include landscaping, painting, adding or improving shutters, lawn care, updating the mailbox, property address numbers, or exterior lighting. These upgrades can attract higher-paying tenants and increase the property's value. This approach is also common in value-add strategies or the BRRRR (Buy, Rehab, Rent, Refinance, Repeat) method, where the goal is to improve the property to increase its rent and overall profitability.
- **Solar** - Installing solar panels and including the cost of electricity in the base rent can make your property more attractive to tenants who value energy efficiency,

potentially allowing you to charge higher rents. However, you should be cautious about the legal implications of charging for utilities, as this can sometimes enter a gray area. It's advisable to consult with a local attorney to ensure compliance with utility billing regulations.

- **Furnished Rental** - Offering a furnished rental can significantly increase the rent you can charge, especially if you shift your strategy to short-term or medium-term rentals, such as vacation rentals, student rentals, or corporate housing. Furnished rentals appeal to tenants looking for convenience and are often willing to pay a premium for a move-in ready home.

- **Convert Property** - Converting a single-family property into a duplex, triplex, or fourplex can increase your rental income by creating multiple rental units within the same property. This approach is especially effective if the property is already somewhat set up for such a conversion. However, it may be cost-prohibitive or even impossible if significant structural changes are required or if zoning laws restrict such conversions. Always check with your city and county regarding zoning and licensing requirements before starting any conversion work, as this can also affect the types of loans you can secure and their terms, including the loan-to-value ratio.

- **Improvement Rent** - Charging extra rent for specific property improvements can help offset the cost of upgrades while increasing your overall rental income. For example, you might charge a tenant more for installing new carpet or a fence. While you may not be able to recoup the full cost of the improvement from a single tenant, some upgrades, like a fence, can justify higher rents with future tenants as well, allowing you to gradually recover your investment and potentially earn a return. This strategy is particularly useful for items with a long lifespan, where the cost can be spread out over multiple tenancies.

While property improvements can significantly boost your rental income, the way you market your property can be equally important for maximizing cash flow. By implementing effective marketing strategies, you can attract high-quality tenants, reduce vacancy periods, and potentially command higher rents. Let's explore some key strategies for improving cash flow through smart marketing techniques.

Marketing the Property for Rent

Here are the cash flow improving strategies to implement while you're marketing your property for rent.

- **Optimize Marketing** - Effective marketing starts with high-quality materials. Ensure that you have professional-grade photos, a 3D tour, and a video to showcase your property. These elements can significantly enhance the appeal of your listing, attracting more potential tenants. Additionally, use online marketing as well as flyers and signs strategically around the neighborhood to increase visibility. Well-designed marketing materials make your property stand out and convey a sense of professionalism that can justify higher rent and reduce vacancy periods.

- **Maximize Exposure** - To attract the right tenants, it's crucial to advertise your property across all available platforms where tenants might be searching. This includes online rental websites, social media, and community bulletin boards. Physical advertising, such as yard signs and directional signs leading to the property, can also capture the attention of local renters. By maximizing exposure, you increase the chances of filling vacancies quickly and with quality tenants.
- **Sales Skills** - Mastering sales skills is essential for renting your property at the highest possible rate and minimizing vacancy. This includes both phone skills for initial inquiries and in-person salesmanship during property tours. Being persuasive and knowledgeable helps you connect with potential tenants, address their concerns, and highlight the property's best features, ultimately leading to faster lease agreements and better tenant retention.
- **Optimize Showings** - Preparing your property for showings is a key step in securing a lease. Ensure the property is well-lit, smells pleasant, and is clean, neat, and in good repair. First impressions matter, and a well-presented property can make the difference between a potential tenant choosing your property over another. Additionally, create a sense of scarcity by scheduling back-to-back showings and mentioning this when booking appointments. This strategy can create urgency and increase interest among prospective tenants.

While effective marketing strategies can help attract tenants and maximize rental income, it's equally important to focus on optimizing your property's financial performance during ownership. Let's explore various strategies you can implement to improve cash flow throughout your tenure as a property owner.

While Owning the Property

Here are the cash flow improving strategies to implement while you own the property.

Refi/Pay Off Loan

Managing your mortgage can be one of the most effective ways to improve cash flow and overall property profitability.

- **Refi to Extend Term** - If your loan is old enough, consider refinancing to extend the loan term. This can lower your monthly payments and—if interest rates have dropped and/or your loan-to-value has improved—potentially secure a better interest rate, improving your cash flow.
- **Refi to Improve Rate** - If interest rates have dropped since you first took out your mortgage, refinancing to a lower rate can reduce your monthly payments and save you money over the life of the loan.
- **Payoff Loan** - If you have the financial means, paying off your loan in its entirety can eliminate your mortgage payments, drastically improving your monthly cash flow and reducing financial stress.

Taxes

Property taxes are a significant expense for any property owner, and managing them effectively can save you money.

- **Correct Assessor** - Ensure that the county assessor has accurate information about your property's condition and characteristics. Correcting any inaccuracies can prevent overvaluation and keep your taxes in check.
- **Contest Tax Increases** - If your property taxes increase, consider contesting the increase. Successful challenges can lead to reduced tax bills and improved cash flow.
- **Vote** - Participate in local elections and vote on measures that affect property taxes. Being informed and voting appropriately can help control future tax increases.

Insurance

Insurance is essential for protecting your investment, but it's also an area where you can manage costs.

- **Shop Insurance Rates** - Regularly compare insurance rates from different providers to ensure you're getting the best deal. Competitive rates can lower your insurance costs without sacrificing coverage.
- **Insurance Coverage** - Review your property insurance policy to make sure you have the right level of coverage. Avoid overpaying for unnecessary coverage or underinsuring your property. It is not just about

minimizing this cost while sacrificing coverage; you must make sure you minimize cost while keeping a desirable level of coverage. Sacrificing coverage is short-sighted and might significantly hurt cash flow if you ever have a claim that is you opted not to cover.

- **Insured** - Adjust your insurance policy by adding or removing people as needed to optimize your rates. This can lead to lower premiums.
- **Insurance Deductible** - Consider raising your deductible to lower your insurance premium. Taking on more risk personally can reduce your monthly insurance costs. See comments about sacrificing coverage being short-sighted above.
- **Remove PMI** - Totally different type of insurance, but if your property's equity has increased sufficiently, you may be able to remove Private Mortgage Insurance (PMI). This can significantly reduce your monthly mortgage payment.

Making Payments

How you manage your payments can also impact your overall costs.

- **Discount for Autopay** - Sign up for autopay on utilities and other bills to avoid per-bill fees. Many service providers offer small discounts or waive fees for customers who enroll in autopay.
- **Discount for Early Payments** - Some service providers, such as HOA or insurance companies, offer

discounts for early payments. Paying these bills in advance can reduce your overall expenses.

Management

Whether you manage your property yourself or hire a professional, effective management is key to maintaining profitability.

- **Self-Manage** - If you choose to manage the property yourself, ensure you stay up to date with the latest laws, best practices, and compliance issues. Self-management can save on property management fees, but it often requires a significant time investment.
- **Professional Property Manager** - Shop around for a high-quality property manager who offers reasonable fees. A good property manager can maximize your rental income and minimize headaches.
- **Manage the Manager** - Even with a professional property manager, it's important to regularly review management statements for accuracy. Mistakes can happen, and catching them early can save you money.
- **Insist on Best Practices** - Ensure your property manager follows best practices, such as marketing your property early and raising rents with each lease renewal. This proactive approach can help maximize your rental income.

Maintenance

Regular maintenance is crucial for keeping your property in good condition and minimizing vacancies.

- **Maintain Property** - Regularly maintaining your property can reduce the time it spends vacant between tenants. A well-maintained property attracts tenants quickly and reduces downtime.
- **Quality Materials** - Using quality materials for maintenance and repairs may have a higher upfront cost, but it can lower the overall cost of maintenance over time by reducing the frequency of repairs and replacements.

Depreciation

Depreciation can provide significant tax benefits, and managing it strategically can enhance your investment returns.

- **Accelerate Depreciation** - Consider accelerating depreciation on your property to maximize tax benefits in the short term. This strategy can improve your cash flow by reducing your taxable income, but it should be used with careful planning to avoid potential future tax liabilities. This can be one of the larger improvements to your cash flow.

While the strategies for improving cash flow during property ownership are crucial, it's equally important to optimize your rental income while renting it. Let's explore various techniques you can implement to enhance your cash flow during the rental phase of your investment.

While Renting the Property

Here are the cash flow improving strategies to implement while you're renting the property.

Add Services

Offering additional services can increase rental income and enhance tenant satisfaction.

- **Additional Services** - Consider offering additional services such as high-speed internet, cable, or utilities for an extra fee. Tenants often value the convenience of bundled services, making this an effective way to boost your rental income. However, be sure to check local laws, as this practice may not be permitted in some areas.
- **DFY Services** - Offer done-for-you (DFY) services such as lawn care, snow removal, or house cleaning. These services can be billed as extras, appealing to tenants who prefer convenience and are willing to pay for it.

Charge Appropriately

Setting appropriate charges can maximize your rental income while offering flexibility to tenants.

- **Bill Back** - Implement bill-back strategies for utilities or HOA services, such as charging tenants for non-potable water or other shared resources. This helps to ensure that tenants are covering their fair share of costs, improving your net income.
- **Tier Rent by Credit Score** - Adjust rent based on the tenant's credit score, with higher rent for those with lower scores. This can also apply to security deposits, where tenants with better credit pay less upfront. Check with your attorney before implementing this strategy.
- **Pet Rent** - Charge additional rent for tenants with pets. Pet rent can help cover potential wear and tear caused by pets and increase your overall rental income.

Convenience Billing

Convenience billing options can make it easier for tenants to pay rent while potentially increasing your revenue.

- **Billing Frequency** - Offer more frequent billing options, such as weekly or biweekly payments, instead of the traditional monthly schedule. This can be attractive to tenants who prefer smaller, more manageable payments but can also produce more cash flow over the same period.
- **Autopay** - Here are conflicting ideas where both options may ultimately improve cash flow. Encourage tenants to enroll in autopay by offering a discount or, conversely, charge a fee for those who do not use autopay. Autopay

can reduce late payments and ensure consistent cash flow.

- **Discount On-Time Payment** - Provide a discount for tenants who pay their rent on time or early, incentivizing prompt payments and reducing the need for late payment penalties.
- **Term** - Adjust the term of rental agreements to fit different rental strategies. Consider offering daily, weekly, or short-term/vacation rentals, which can often command higher rents than traditional monthly leases.

Timing

Optimizing the timing of lease agreements and renewals can minimize vacancies and maximize rental income.

- **Notice** - Require a 60-90 day notice from tenants if they intend not to renew their lease. This provides you with ample time to market the property and secure a new tenant, reducing vacancy periods.
- **Start Early/Test Rent** - Begin marketing the property early, even before the current tenant moves out, and start with a higher rent to test the market. This strategy allows you to adjust pricing based on demand and secure the best possible rental rate.
- **Renew Peak Season** - Align lease renewal dates to end during peak rental seasons, such as spring or summer, when demand is higher. This increases the likelihood of filling the property quickly and possibly at a higher rent.

Miscellaneous

Implementing additional requirements can protect your property and reduce potential liabilities.

- **Renter's Insurance** - Require tenants to carry renter's insurance. This protects both you and the tenant in case of damage to the property or loss of personal belongings, reducing potential conflicts and liabilities.

Conclusion

This guide has explored 94 ways to improve cash flow on rental properties across seven distinct stages of your real estate investing process.

Each stage presents unique opportunities to boost your investment's financial performance, and the cumulative effect of applying these strategies can significantly increase your property's profitability.

By focusing on cash flow improvement at every stage, you can:

- Build a more resilient and profitable real estate portfolio
- Enhance property values—especially for properties where value is driven by the income they generate, such as commercial properties
- Strengthen your ability to secure favorable financing by improving loan-to-value (LTV) and debt service coverage ratios
- Optimize tax benefits

- Accelerate savings for larger down payments and quickly replenish reserves
- Increase tenant satisfaction by enhancing the tenant experience, improving retention rates, and reducing turnover costs

Remember, even small adjustments across multiple areas can compound into substantial gains in your overall returns and financial stability.

Make it a habit to regularly review and implement these strategies, tailoring them to fit your specific properties and market conditions.

With consistent effort and strategic application, you can transform your rental properties into powerful, cash-generating assets that support your long-term financial goals.

Introduction to Monte Carlo Analysis of Rental Properties

There's a problem with how we've been modeling our investments so far. It is not unique to us. Almost everyone does it wrong.

But, we're going to fix it now.

The issue is the assumptions we've been using and how the real world works.

88

For the analysis we've been doing with *The World's Greatest Real Estate Deal Analysis Spreadsheet*™ (TWGREDAS)—and any other real estate deal analysis spreadsheet—we've used static assumptions.

We might assume that property values are going up by 3% per year. Well, that's not truly a correct representation of reality.

Heck, with the overrides tab in TWGREDAS we may have said, they go up by 3% for the first 3 years and then only 2% thereafter. Better, but still not reality.

The truth is: we really don't know how much property values will go up as we hold the property. They could go up by 3%. They could go down by 3%. They could go up then down or down then up. Could be more or less than 3%. Might be 3.1% or 2.9%. Might be up or down 6% or 10%.

If we look back at history (and we do when we consider the risks of investing in real estate), we can see what property appreciation has done over the last 100 years.

Risk Matrix: Appreciation

	Severity				
	0	1	2	3	4
Likelihood	Increase	Small Decline	Medium Decline	Large Decline	Catastrophic
1	>10% Increase 7.7%			10-15% Decline 6.0%	>15% Decline 0.0%
2	5-10% Increase 15.0%		5-10% Decline 12.8%		
3	0-5% Increase 25.6%	0-5% Decline 34.6%			

So, to correctly model how our investment might perform, we should not use a static 3% per year—or whatever static number you believe to be true—for property appreciation.

Our crystal balls are broken. We can't accurately predict—exactly—what appreciation will be for our properties.

We can guess. Based on what has happened in the past they will average about 3% per year.

But they may:

- Increase in value by more than 10% for the year about 7.7% of the time
- Increase between 5% and 10% for the year about 15% of the time
- Increase between 0% and 5% for the year about 25.6% of the time
- Go down in value between 0% and 5% for the year about 34.6% of the time

- Go down in value between 5% and 10% for the year about 12.8% of the time
- Go down in value between 10% and 15% for the year about 6% of the time

These are based on what has happened over the last 100 years. Could the future be different? Absolutely.

But it is much more accurate than just assuming that they will be going up in value by 3% per year every year.

Not Just Property Appreciation

As you probably guessed, this isn't just an issue with property appreciation. It applies to other assumptions we have as well.

Here's a list of some of the more significant ones:

- **Property Appreciation Rate** - This is the one we've been talking about already. It is how much properties go up or down in value.
- **Rent Appreciation Rate** - This is how much rents increase or decrease with each lease renewal.
- **Inflation Rate** - Inflation reflects the overall increase in prices and the decrease in purchasing power over time. It impacts everything from the cost of goods and services to the value of money itself. In the context of your portfolio, inflation affects how much your money will be worth in the future, influencing the real returns on your investments. For instance, even if your rental

income and property values rise, high inflation could erode those gains in terms of actual purchasing power. A million dollars today isn't the same as a million dollars 50 years ago and it won't be the same as a million dollars 50 years from now.

- **Mortgage Interest Rates** - **Mortgage Interest Rates** - Mortgage rates fluctuate over time. The rate you secure for your current property purchase or refinance won't necessarily be the same for properties you buy in one, five, or more years from now.
- **Stock Market Rate of Return** - This is how much you're earning on money you have invested in the stock market. This also applies to other investments you might have like savings accounts, bonds, CDs, cryptocurrencies, etc.

If you really want to go to freaky town, you could also model this with changing tax rates, insurance rates, maintenance and capital expenses on the property.

Does This Even Matter?

Does this even matter and why should I care?

Let's start with a simple example of someone who invests in stocks. They don't even buy a home to live in; they rent instead.

They invest approximately 10% of their income in the stock market earning 8% per year.

Using static assumptions, we could calculate that they would be financially independent (FI) after about 53.25 years.

See **Error! Reference source not found.** at the end of the chapter. We moved the charts to the end of the chapter—instead of inline—so we could show you larger, readable versions of the charts.

But what if we used a reasonable range of values for the return from the stock market instead of always 8% every year?

We could use a range of values that better approximates what the stock markets has done historically—still averaging about 8% for this selection of stocks.

Instead of seeing a smooth line showing their journey toward financial independence as shown in Error! Reference source not found. at the end of the chapter.

We'd instead see a less smooth line representing how the stock market returns change each month like Error! Reference source not found..

And, if we ran it 10 times, you'd see that when they actually achieve financial independence (when the line crosses the horizontal dotted line) is a little different each time. See Error! Reference source not found..

If the stock market performs well, they're financially independent earlier. If the stock market does not perform as well, they end up being financially independent later.

If we ran this 1,000 times and summarized the results, we can see the range of when they're financially independent. See Error! Reference source not found..

Monte Carlo Modeling

This type of analysis is called Monte Carlo modeling.

Monte Carlo modeling is a statistical technique used to simulate multiple potential outcomes for an investment or financial scenario.

It works by:

- Running hundreds or thousands of simulations with varying input parameters
- Analyzing the range and probability of different outcomes
- Providing a more nuanced understanding of potential risks and returns

For real estate investing, Monte Carlo analysis involves varying input factors such as property appreciation rates, rent increases, mortgage interest rates, inflation, and market returns. This approach allows you to better assess the likelihood of achieving your financial goals and understand the potential risks associated with your investment strategies.

I like to call it *Alternate Universe Modeling*™ because we're consider how your investments might perform if you were living in alternate universes with different futures.

Back to our example with someone just investing in stocks.

In Error! Reference source not found. at the end of the chapter:

- The light blue band shows the full range of results from the very worst to the very best.
- The darker blue band in the middle shows you the middle 50% of all runs. Half of the time the results are this darker band.
- The dark link at the very center shows you the median value. Half the values are higher than this. Half the values are lower than this.

If we look at the median line we can see that half the time they're financially independent around 58 years. Half the time it is after 58 years.

It could have been as early as year 48. And, it could take longer than 60 years—when we stopped modeling for this example. In fact, only about 85% of the 1,000 runs we ran were financially independent 60 years from when they started.

We can summarize this is a different chart and show what percentage of the 1,000 runs were financially independent in each month. That's Error! Reference source not found..

By using a range of values for things like the stock market rate of return, we get a much more nuanced understanding of what is likely to happen.

What If They Became Homeowners Instead of Renting?

Our last example they were renting a property to live in and investing in stocks.

What if they bought on owner-occupant property with 5% down to live in and invested in stocks?

If we used static assumptions they would be financially independent about 15 and half years faster as shown in Error! Reference source not found. at the end of the chapter.

Part of what gets them to financial independence faster is that they end up paying off their owner-occupant property 30 years after they buy it. Without a mortgage payment the threshold for them being financially independent is a little lower.

There's a little more to this story, but I don't want to go off into the weeds here. The punchline is they achieve financial independence faster with static assumptions as you can see in Error! Reference source not found..

Let's vary the property appreciation rate, mortgage interest rate, inflation rate, and stock market rate of return. If we were discussing rentals, we'd vary the rent appreciation rate as well but in this case they're not buying any rentals; we'll get to that shortly.

96

With variable property appreciation rates, mortgage interest rates until they lock in a 30-year fixed rate financing loan, inflation rate and stock market rate of return it looks like Error! Reference source not found..

They're financially independent as early as 33.75 years from when they start. In 99.5% of the 1,000 runs they're financially independent by the time we stop modeling at 60 years.

How does this compare to them just investing in stocks? Let's show both on one chart in Error! Reference source not found..

Buying an owner-occupant property seems to make a pretty big difference.

If we just look at what percentage of the 1,000 runs they achieve financial independence, you can see that buying the owner-occupant property is more probable (higher percentage of the runs achieve it) and they're financially independent earlier (it happens more to the left on the chart). See Error! Reference source not found..

Buying Rental Properties with 20% Down Payments

Let's assume, for now, that they don't buy an owner-occupant property with 5% down. Instead, they decide to buy 20% down rental properties as their primary investing strategy.

Any additional money beyond what they need for the rentals is still investing in stocks, but whenever they get enough for a 20% down payment they buy a rental property with very modest cash flow.

They're willing to buy up to ten 20% down payment rentals.

If we have **static assumptions** for property appreciation, rent appreciation, inflation, mortgage interest rates and the stock market rate of return, they might be financially independent after 31 years.

With static assumptions, that's about 18.67 years faster than just investing in stocks and about 3 years faster than buying an owner-occupant property and investing stocks as shown in Error! Reference source not found..

With static assumptions, they achieve financial independence faster. See Error! Reference source not found..

And, still looking at the chart above, they appear have a lot more income coming then just investing in stocks the longer they hold the rental properties.

In fact, they're earning about twice what they need to be financially independent about 48.5 years in. That means they're earning twice what they need to be financially independent before just investing in stocks as a renter is even earning enough for them to financially independent at all.

98

Not long after they achieve financial independence just investing in stocks as a renter, they're earning 3 times what they need to be financially independent with their 10 rentals.

But, this is about Monte Carlo modeling, so what if we did vary property appreciation rates, rent appreciation rates, inflation, mortgage interest rates and the stock market rate of return?

It is important to realize that because the property prices vary with each run sometimes the properties they're buying can be slightly more or less expensive. On average though, property prices are going up at about 3% per year.

Rent is similar. Rents can go up or down, but overall, rents are increasing by about 3% per year.

Mortgage interest rates started at about 8.5% for a non-owner-occupant loan without paying significant points. But, mortgage interest rates can get better—or worse—over time as they're acquiring properties. That means sometimes properties will cash flow better and sometimes they'll cash flow a little worse.

Let's look at their journey to financial independence buying ten 20% down payment rentals in Error! Reference source not found..

You can see there are times when the market goes in their favor (both the real estate and stock market) they achieve financial independence early. And, there are times when they still don't quite achieve it through 60 years.

How does it compare to the two previous strategies: renting and investing exclusively in stocks and buying an owner-occupant property and exclusively investing in stocks? See Error! Reference source not found..

It is getting harder to see what is happening in the chart as we add additional comparisons.

We can make it easier in two different ways. First, we can look at the same chart, but turn off the shaded areas for each strategy.

This would leave just the median—or the middle-most result—where half of them are better and half are worse. That's Error! Reference source not found..

This chart doesn't show up the range of results (how early or late they achieve FI) but it does show how much more they're likely to earn by buying the rentals by what percent of their financial independence goal they're earning.

By earning a higher percentage of the amount they need to be financially independent, they're able to support a higher standard of living.

In other words, if they needed to be earning $10,000 per month passively to be considered financially independent, but their earning 200% of that—or $20,000 per month—they could live at a much higher standard of living on $20,000 per month than the $10,000 per month that they needed—at a minimum—to be considered financially independent.

The second way to make it easier to see what is happening is looking at the percentage of the 1,000 runs that achieved financial independence like we did previously. That's Error! Reference source not found..

Buying ten 20% down payment rentals sees them achieving financial independence earlier (more left on the chart above) and then has a similar success rate to what they'd see if they bought an owner-occupant and invested in stocks.

Owner-Occupant, Rentals and Stocks

I think you know what's coming next: what if they bought an owner-occupant property with 5% down, then bought up to nine more rental properties, each with 20% down payments and invested the rest in stocks?

With static assumptions that's about 3.5 years faster than just renting and buying ten 20% down payment rentals. See Error! Reference source not found..

If we do Monte Carlo modeling, it looks like Error! Reference source not found..

Doing a very busy version of this chart by comparing it to the other strategies so far, it looks like Error! Reference source not found..

If we just look at the 50th percentile (median) value for the four options as seen in Error! Reference source not found..

It shows that buying the owner-occupant property and nine 20% down payment rentals appears to be faster and gives them a higher standard of living than even buying ten 20% down payment rentals.

If we look at the percentage of the 1,000 runs for reach strategy that achieved financial independence and when, we can see that buying an owner-occupant property and then nine 20% down rentals is the best performer yet as seen in Error! Reference source not found..

In the chart above you can see that not only does financial independence tend to happen faster (a little to the left on the chart), it also tends to be more consistent (a higher percentage of the runs achieve FI).

Nomad™ Real Estate Investing Strategy Example

There's so much more we could do with this, but for now I'll wrap it up with a slight curve ball.

Instead of buying an owner-occupant property and then buying nine 20% down payment rentals, let's imagine they Nomad™.

- They buy an owner-occupant property with 5% down payment.
- They live there for *at least* a year. That's a requirement of the lender to get an owner-occupant loan with an owner-occupant down payment and owner-occupant mortgage interest rate.

- Once their year is up AND they've saved up enough for another 5% down payment, they buy another owner-occupant property and move into it.
- They take the previous property they were living in and convert it to a rental property
- They repeat this until they have 9 rentals and the property they're living in

Instead of having to save up for 20% down payments, they acquire the same nine rental properties with only 5% down on each by moving into each one as an owner-occupant.

Is this better? Is this more probable for them to be financially independent? Is this faster to financial independence? Does this give a higher standard of living than the other strategies so far? And—we won't cover it here because it is a longer discussion—but is it more or less risky?

It turns out that with static assumptions (not Monte Carlo modeling yet), Nomad™ is 58 months (almost 5 years) faster to financial independence. See Error! Reference source not found..

If we add variability and do Monte Carlo modeling, we can look at how the Nomad™ strategy performs in Error! Reference source not found..

Brace yourself for the busy version comparing them all at the same time in Error! Reference source not found..

And, if we turn off the range of results and just look at the middle most (median) of the 1,000 runs for each strategy, we can see the following in Error! Reference source not found..

Still a bit busy to see what is going on, but I will point out, in the chart above, the Nomad™ strategy seems to give them the fastest achievement of financial independence and highest standard of living.

Isn't it interesting.

If we look at the percentage of the 1,000 runs that achieve financial independence and by when you can see even better in Error! Reference source not found..

The Nomad™ strategy achieves financial independence earliest (to the left on the chart above). It also has a higher probability of being financially independent earlier.

Additional Modeling

Now that we know the importance of considering the variability that might occur in the future, this is really just the beginning.

There is a ridiculous amount more to dig into here. We've just barely scratched the surface.

There's a lot more to model.

For example, we could model each strategy you're considering seeing how each strategy performs:

- Buying long-term buy and hold rental properties (short-term rentals, medium-term rentals, student rentals, storage units, assisted living, apartments, etc)

- Buying properties utilizing creative financing (owner financing, wrap financing, loan assumptions, rent-to-owns, agreements for deed, subject-to)
- Variations on the Nomad™ strategy (Nomad™ by Proxy, Nomad™ with House Hacking, Nomad™ to Short-Term Rental, Nomad™ with Lease-Option Exits, *The Ultimate Real Estate Agent Retirement Plan™*)
- House Hacking and related strategies
- Short-Term Rentals and related strategies
- Flipping properties and related strategies
- BRRRR and related strategies
- And much, much more

Or, combining one or more of these strategies at the same time (fix and flipping while acquiring long-term or short-term rentals as an example) or sequentially (fix and flipping for 10 years then switch to buy and hold).

Or, we could test a wide assortment of variations to your strategy:

- More or less reserves (and its impact on both speed and risk)
- More or less down payment size up to buying properties for all cash
- Buying down interest rates or not
- Getting roommates or not (house hacking)
- Selling via lease-options versus with a real estate agent or for sale by owner
- Paying off properties early with extra cash flow versus not

- Doing cash out refinances to buy additional properties faster
- Buying properties and selling them when you could take the proceeds (after all expenses including taxes) and then investing that money in stocks, bonds or something else to be financially independent
- Buying more properties than you need and selling them to pay off properties when it means you'd be financially independent
- And much, much more

Not Just Financial Independence

When we do these models, it is important to consider more than just how fast you're able to get to financial independence—even though that's what we focused on here.

Sometimes it is about your standard of living once you are financially independent. Some strategies might just barely get you to your minimum required income to be financially independent. While others will give you far more each month than you initially stated you needed allowing you to live at a much higher standard of living than you originally required.

Sometimes, it is about measuring, comparing and ultimately minimizing risks. Some strategies are riskier than others. They might get you to financial independence, on average, 1 year faster, but there's a 20 times greater chance you'll run out of money by pursuing that strategy than another one that gets you to financial independence, on average, a year slower.

That all might be worth considering... especially for your own unique situation.

It is important for you to evaluate your own strategy utilizing Monte Carlo modeling to better understand how to achieve financial independence faster, easier, with higher probability of success, with a higher standard of living and with less overall risk.

Or, if you are going to ignore one or more of those things, deliberately and strategically choosing to ignore them with full knowledge of the consequences.

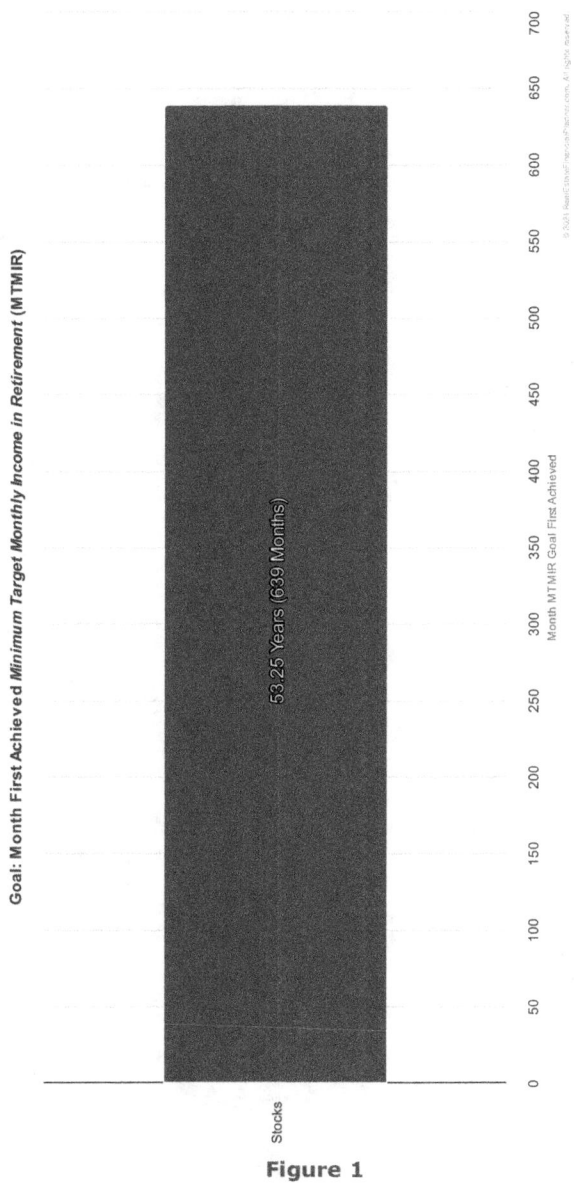

Figure 1

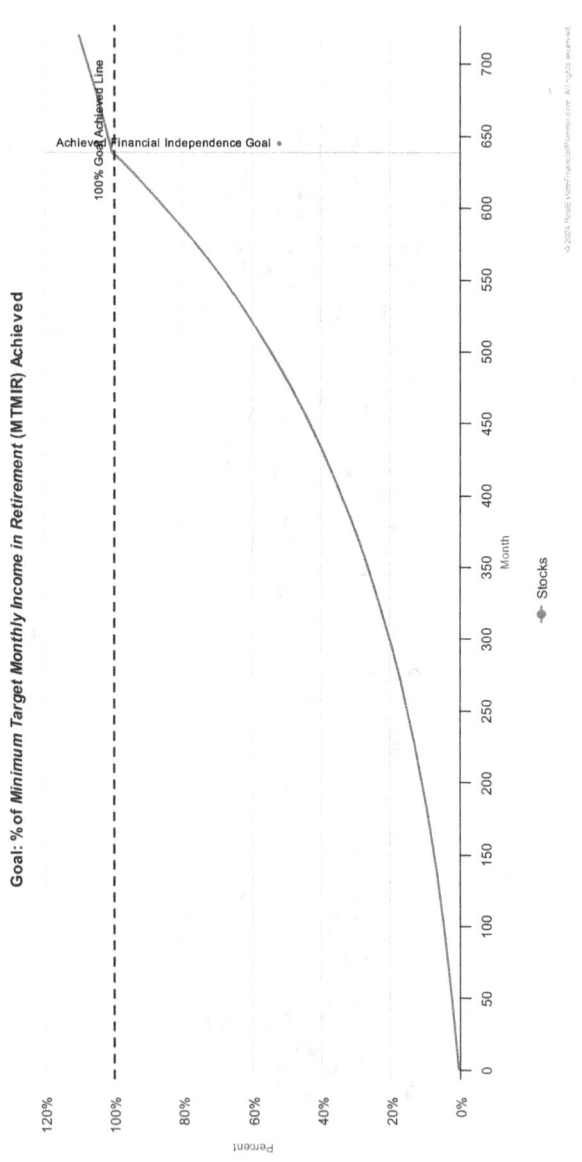

Figure 2

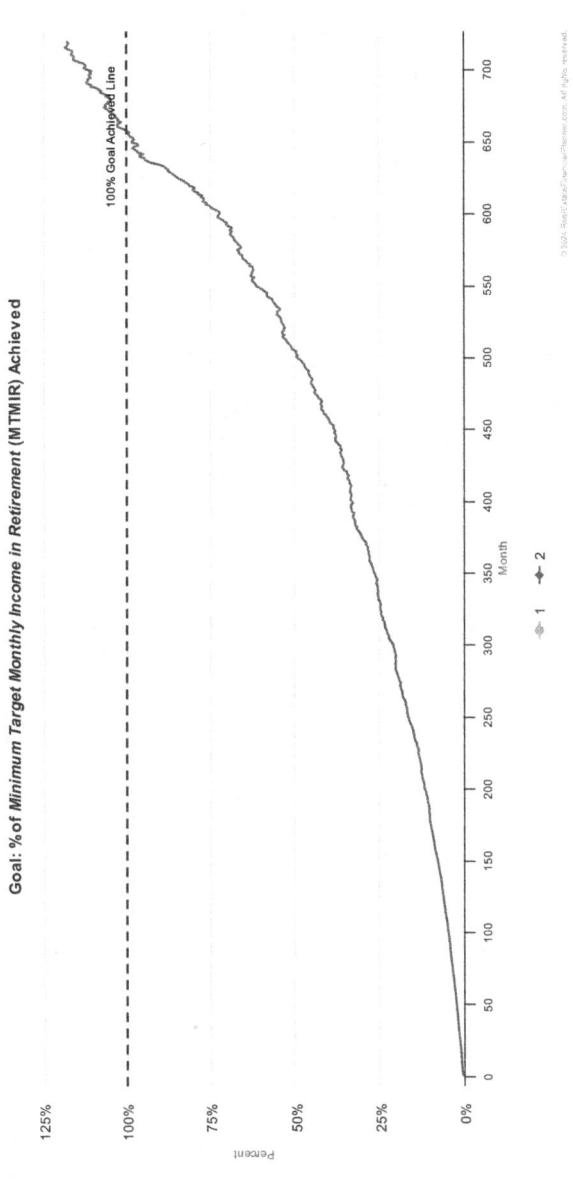

Goal: % of *Minimum Target Monthly Income in Retirement (MTMIR) Achieved*

100% Goal Achieved Line

Month

Percent

1   2

Figure 3

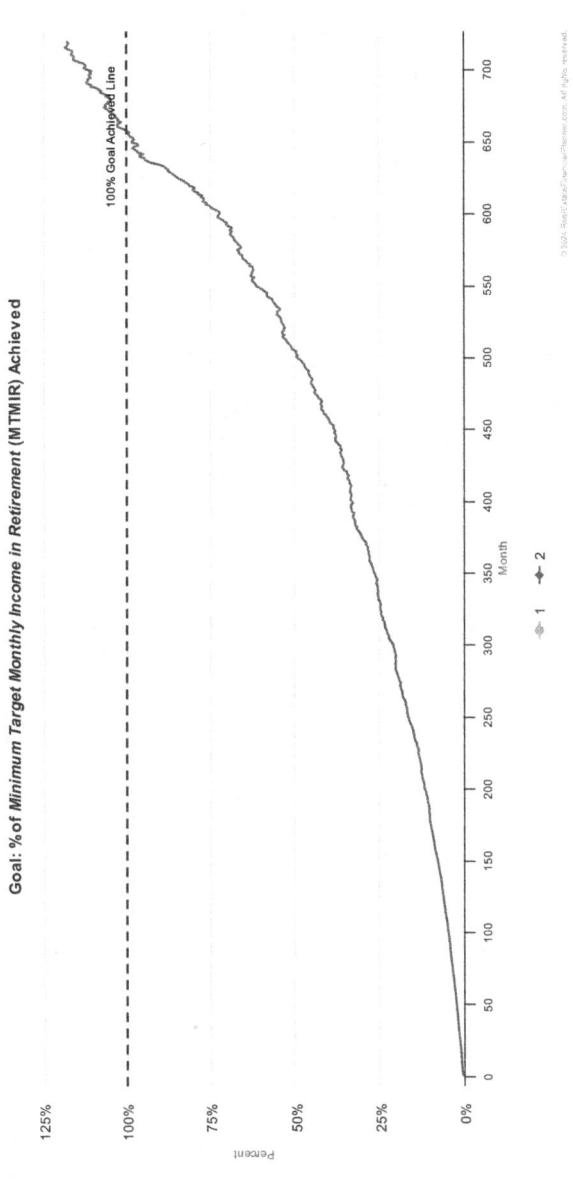

110

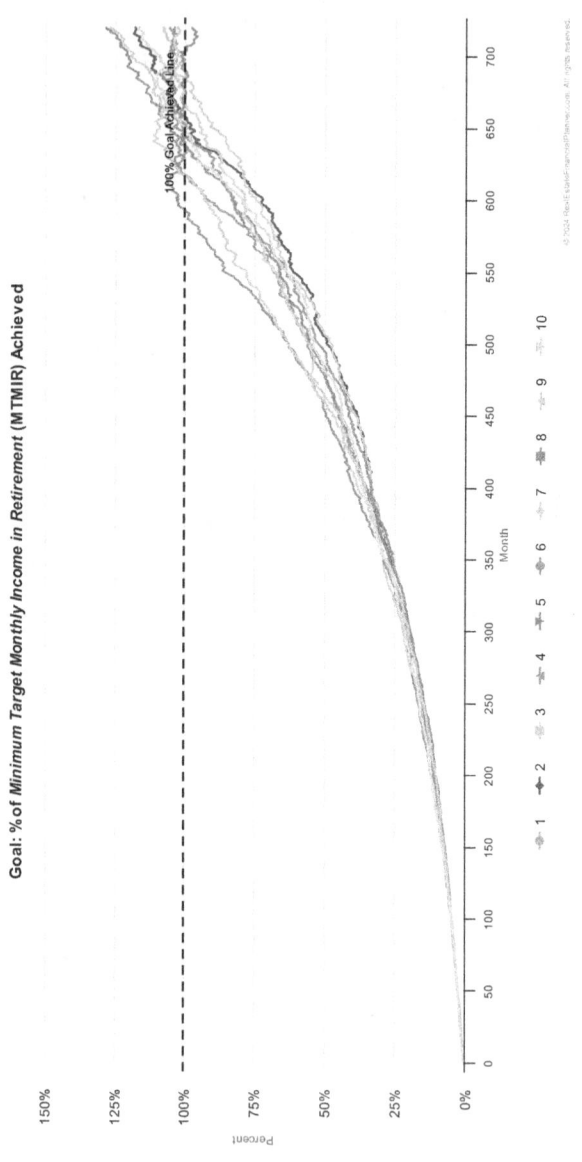

Figure 4

111

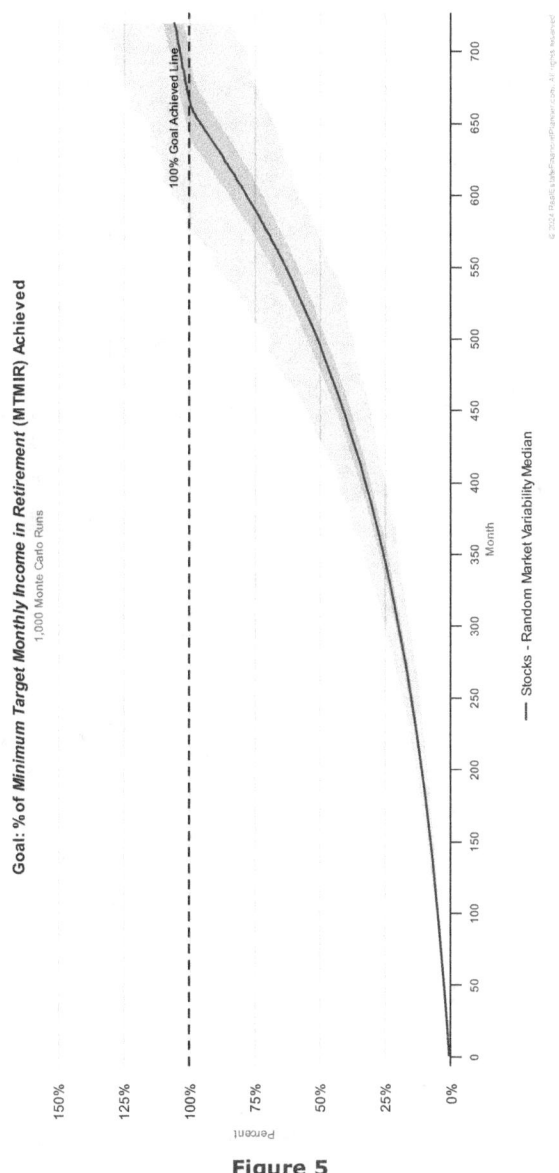

Figure 5

© 2024 James Orr. All rights reserved.

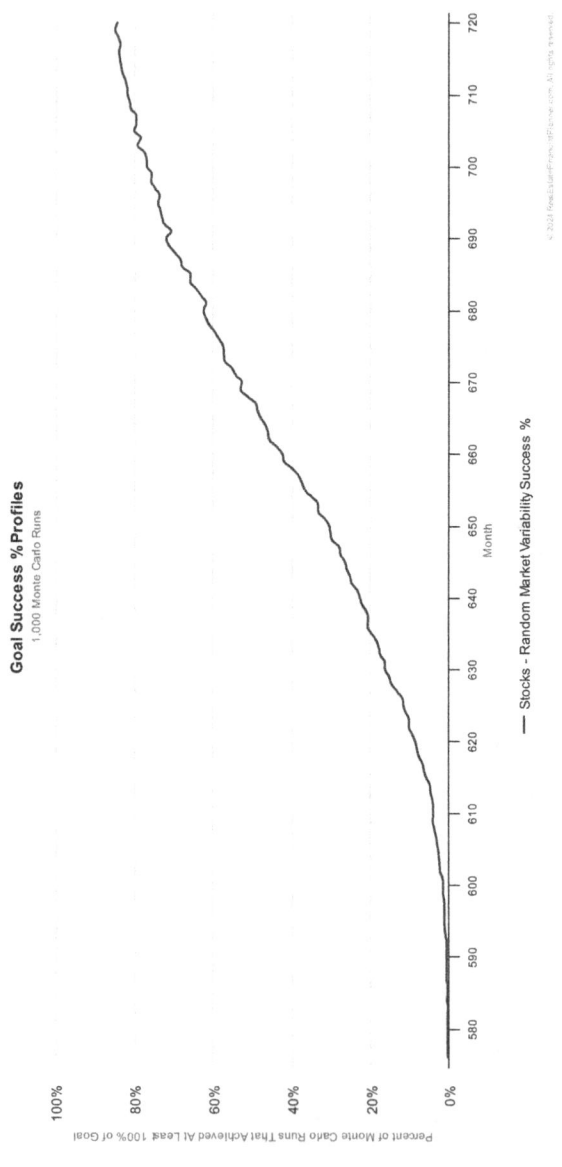

Figure 6

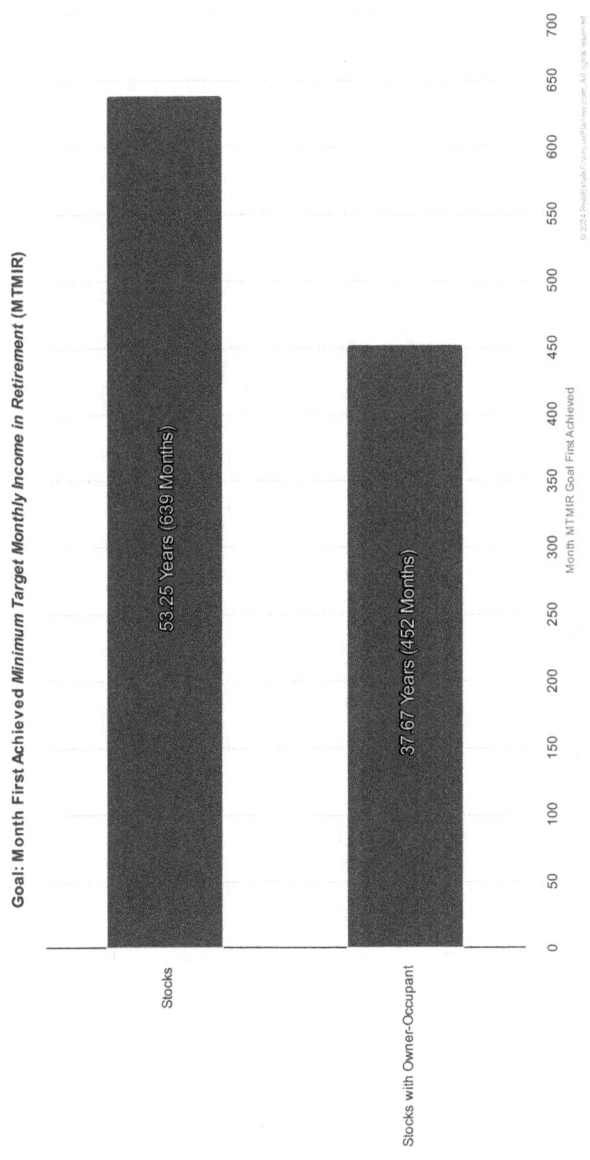

Figure 7

114

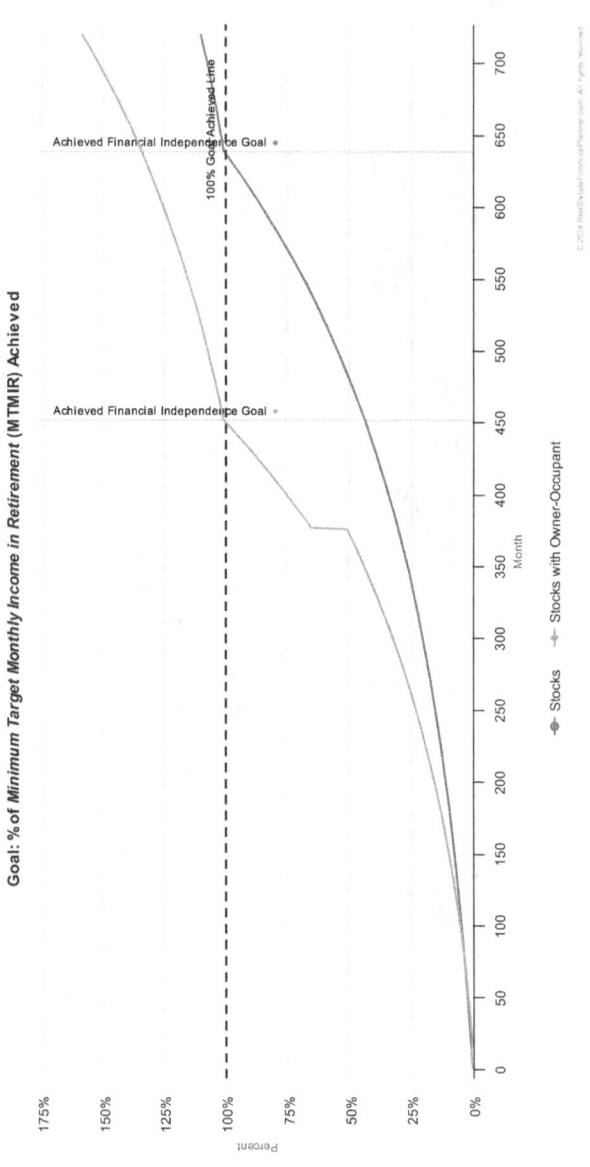

Figure 8

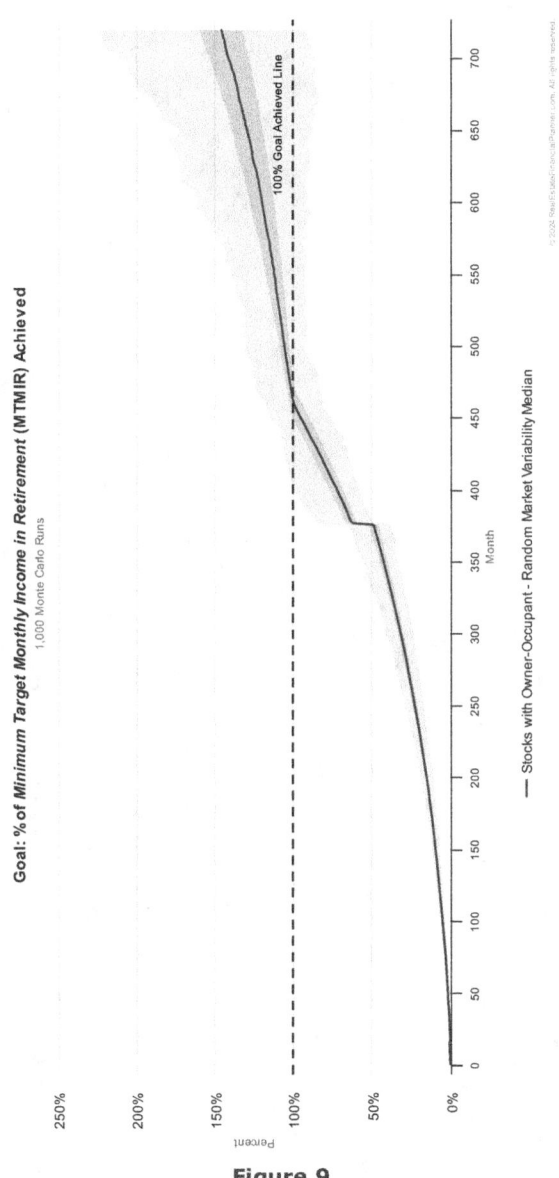

Figure 9

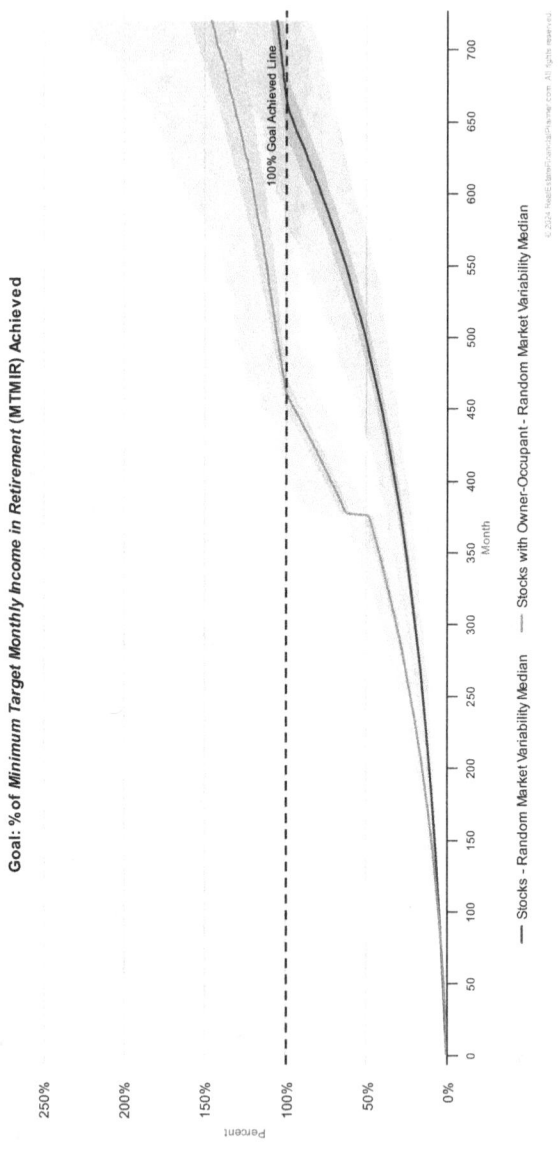

Figure 10

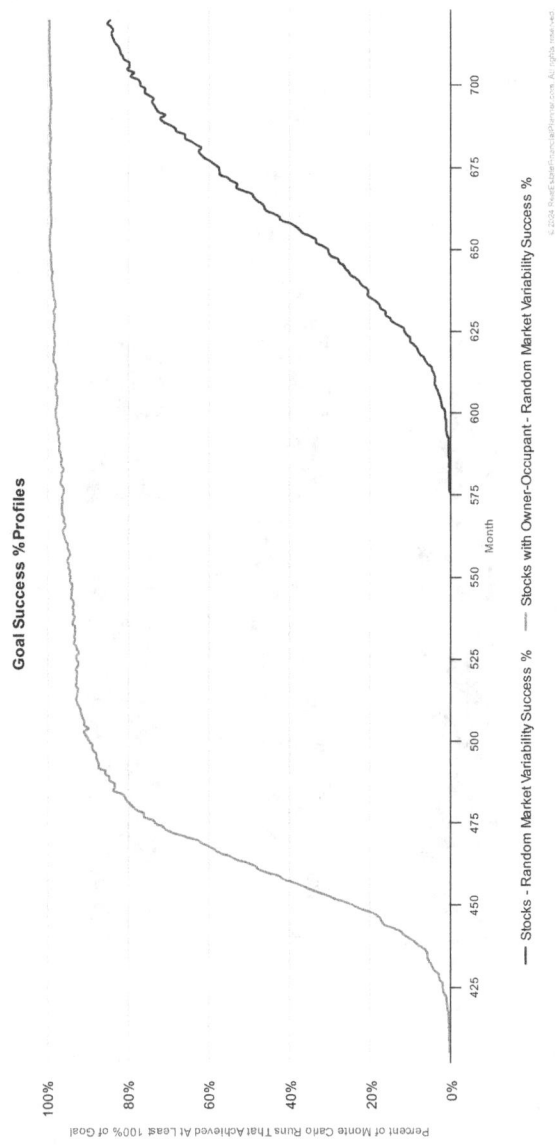

Figure 11

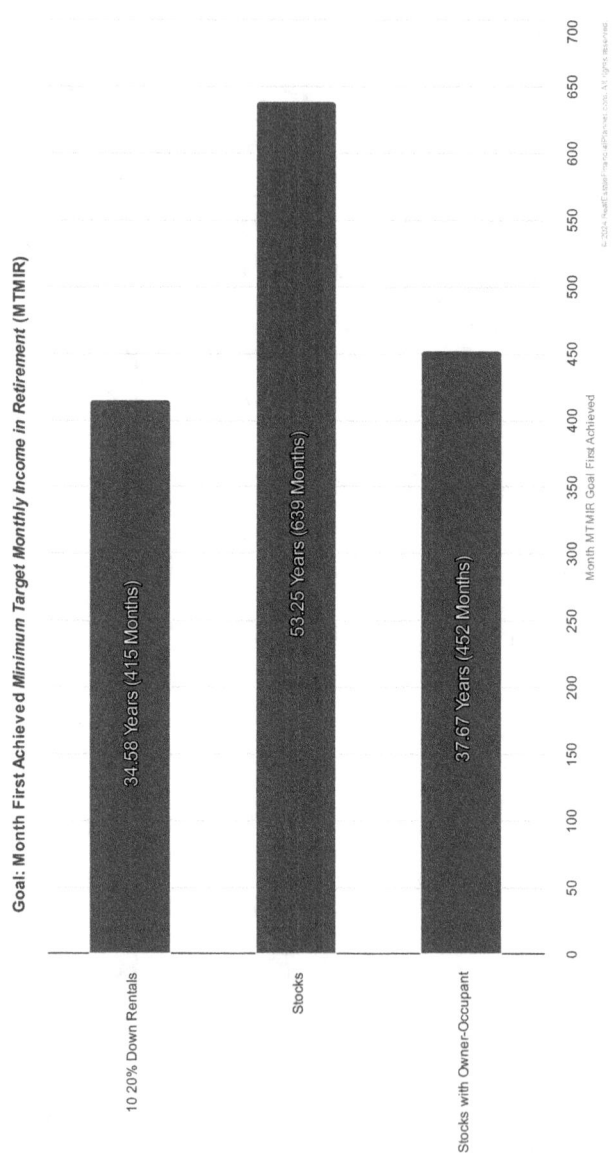

Goal: Month First Achieved *Minimum Target Monthly Income in Retirement* (MTMIR)

Figure 12

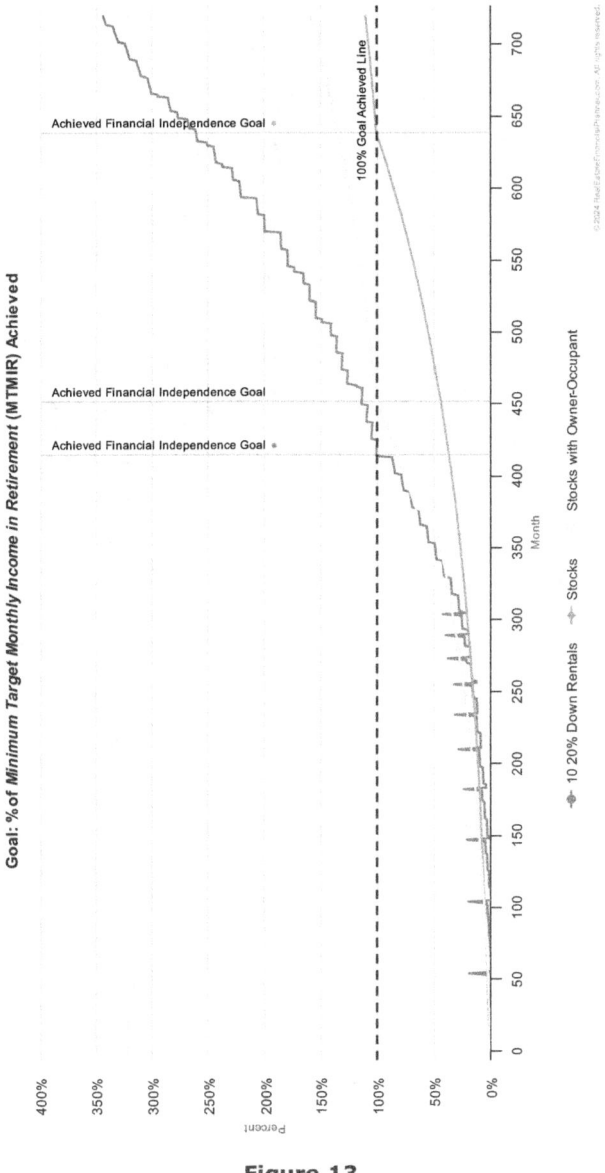

Figure 13

120

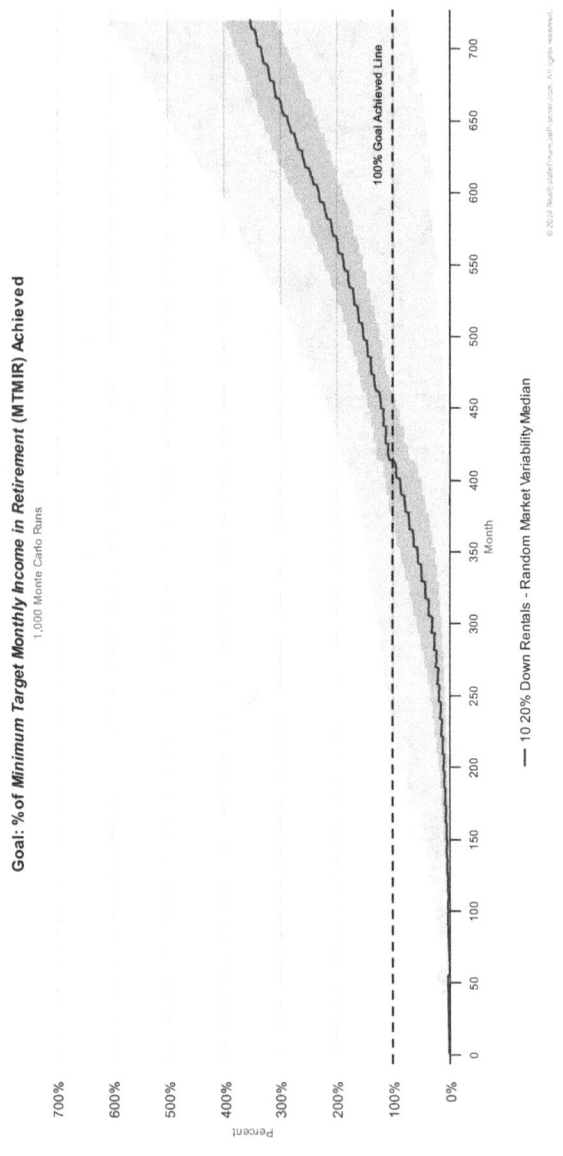

Figure 14

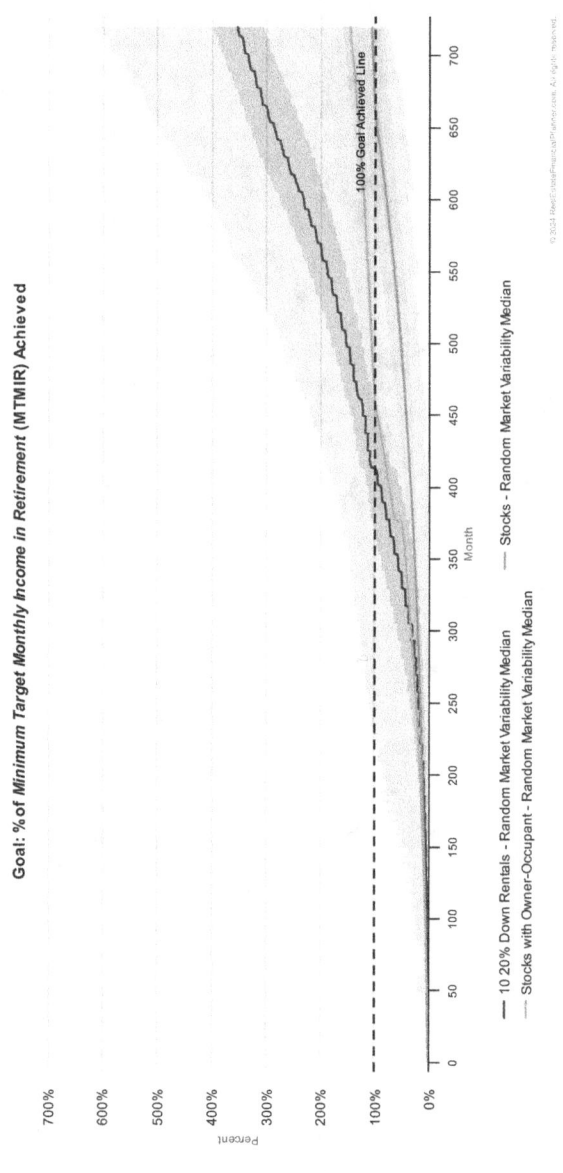

Figure 15

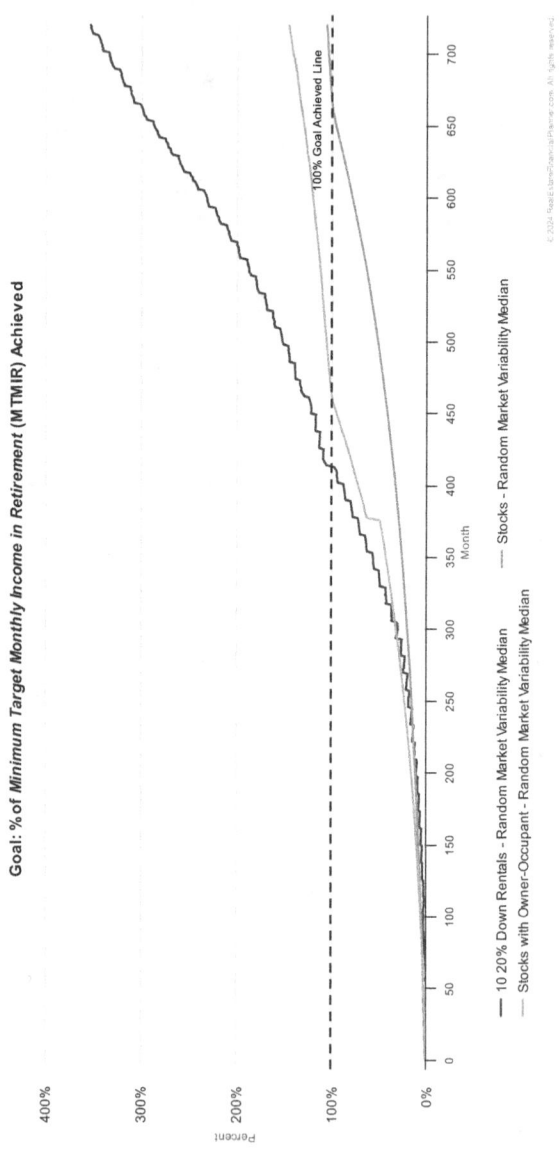

Goal: % of *Minimum Target Monthly Income in Retirement (MTMIR)* Achieved

Figure 16

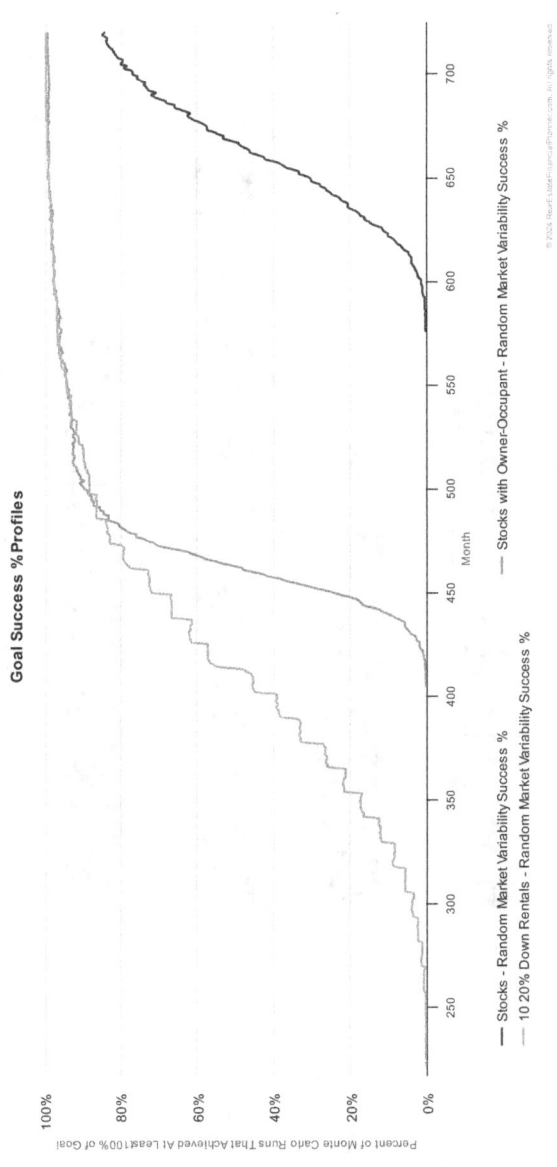

Goal Success % Profiles

— Stocks - Random Market Variability Success %   — Stocks with Owner-Occupant - Random Market Variability Success %
— 10 20% Down Rentals - Random Market Variability Success %

Figure 17

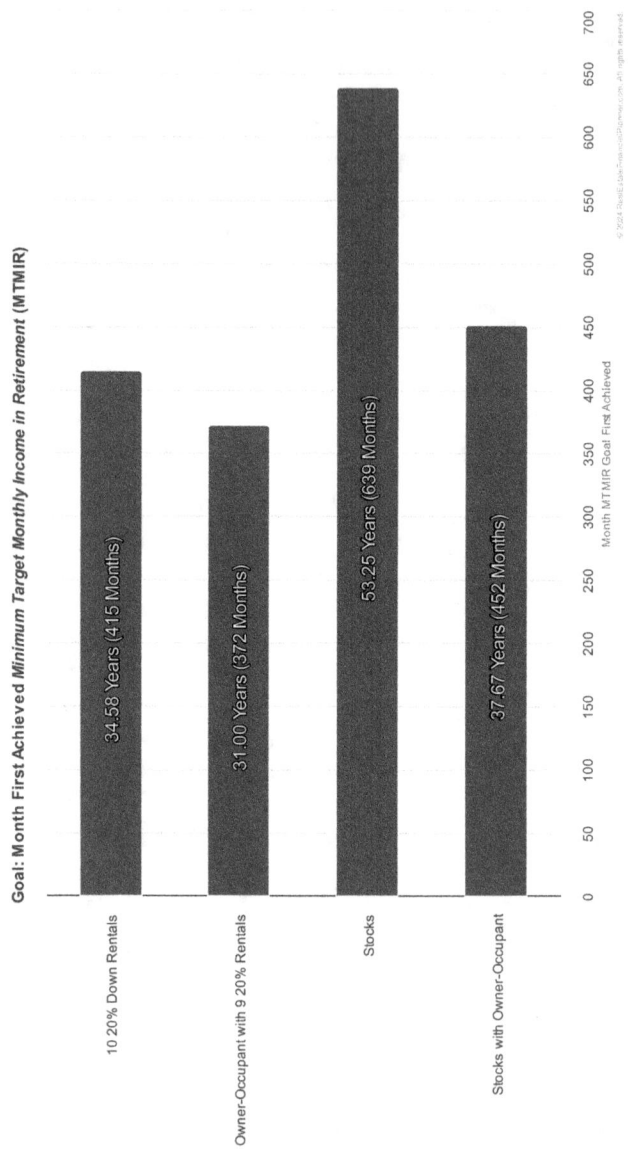

Figure 18

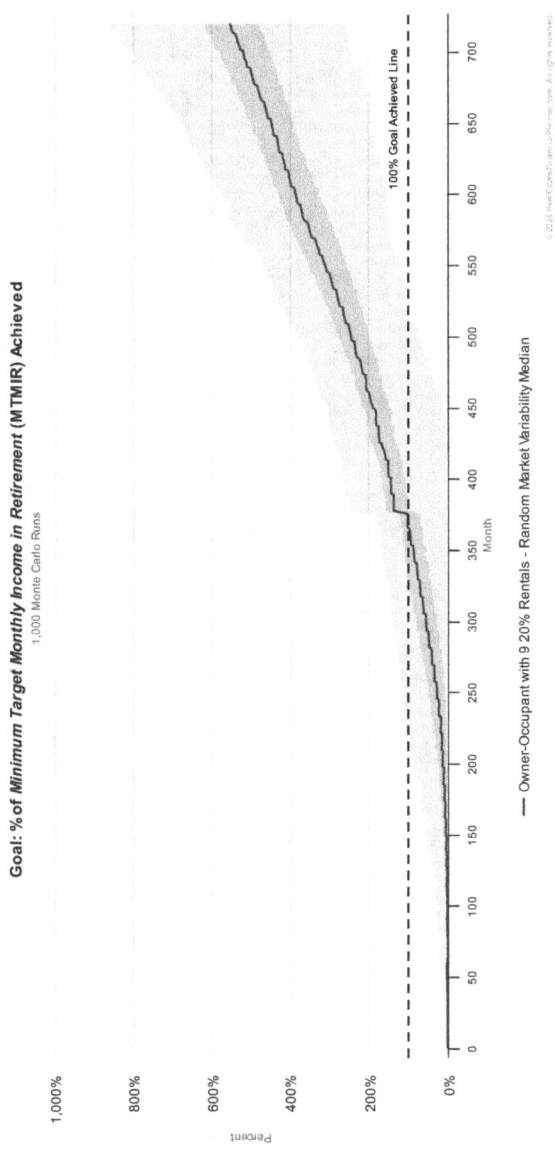

Goal: % of *Minimum Target Monthly Income in Retirement (MTMIR)* Achieved
1,000 Monte Carlo Runs

100% Goal Achieved Line

— Owner-Occupant with 9 20% Rentals - Random Market Variability Median

Figure 19

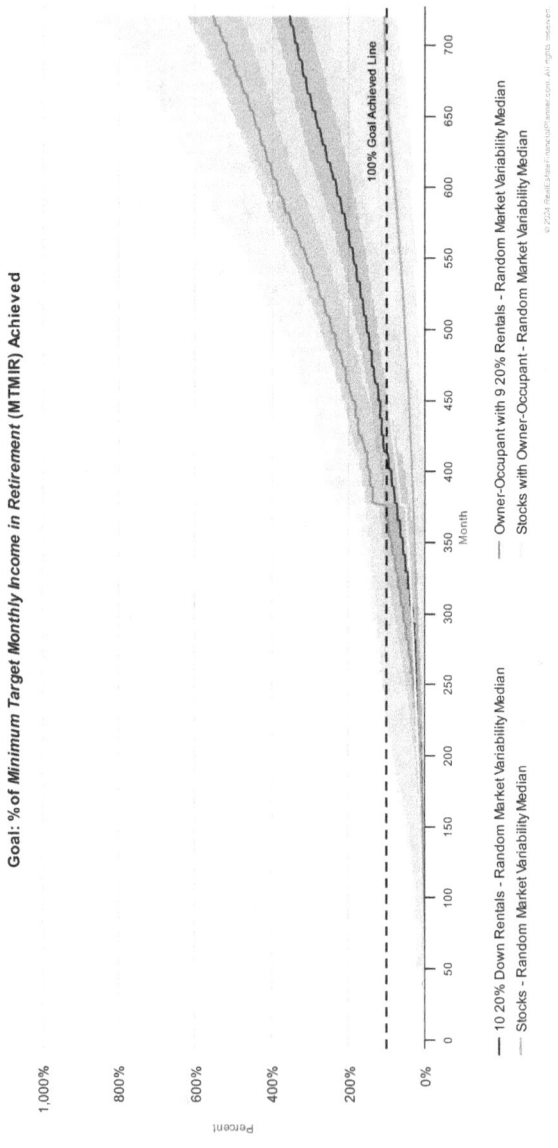

Figure 20

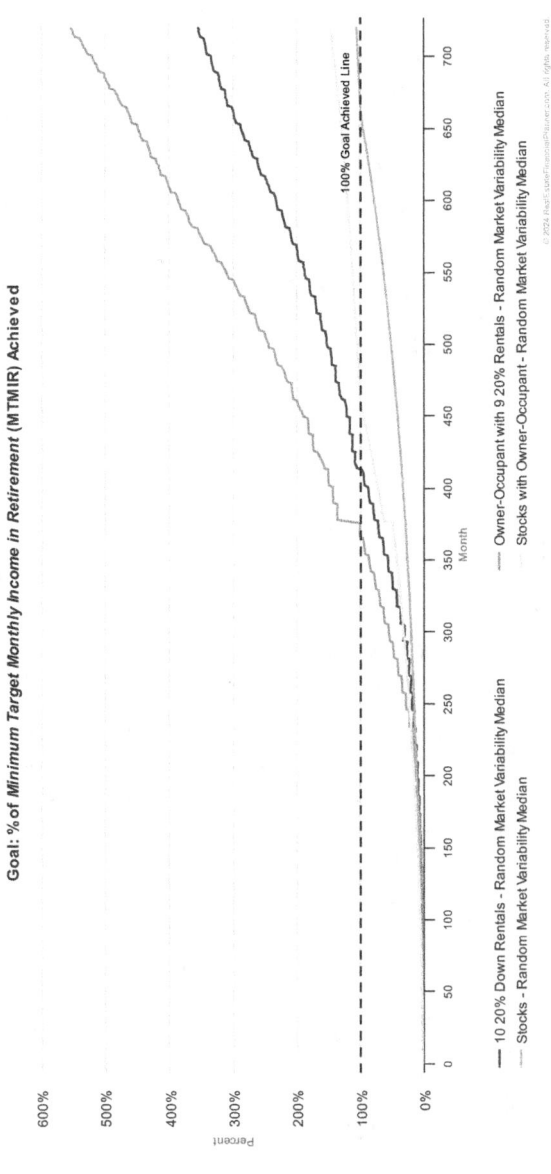

Figure 21

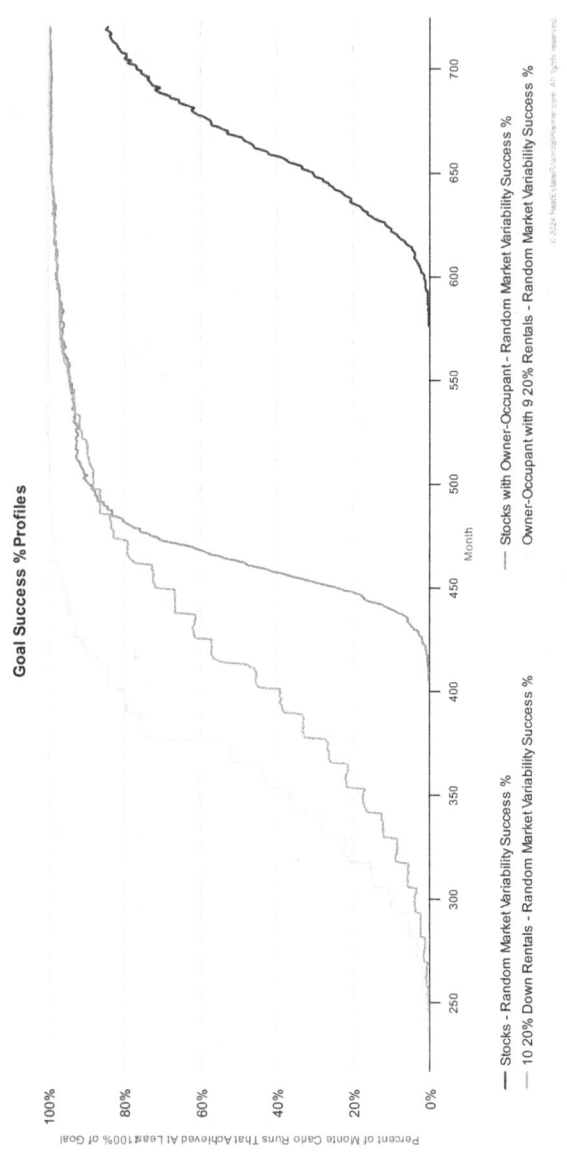

Goal Success % Profiles

Figure 22

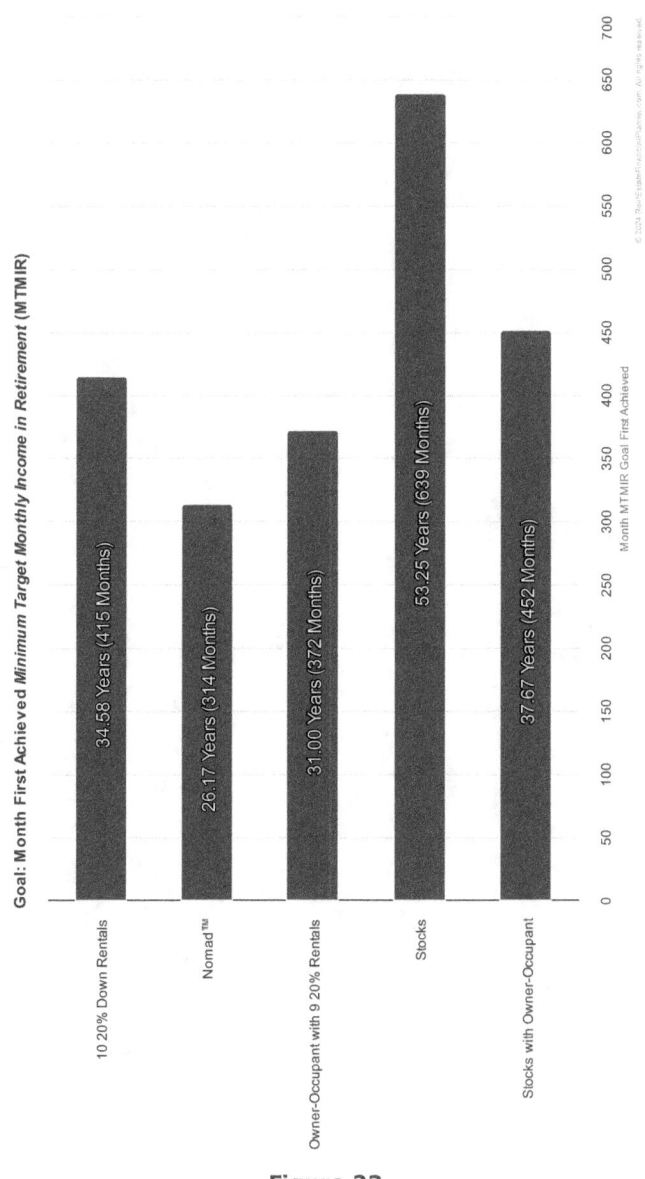

Goal: Month First Achieved Minimum Target Monthly Income in Retirement (MTMIR)

- 10 20% Down Rentals — 34.58 Years (415 Months)
- Nomad™ — 26.17 Years (314 Months)
- Owner-Occupant with 9 20% Rentals — 31.00 Years (372 Months)
- Stocks — 53.25 Years (639 Months)
- Stocks with Owner-Occupant — 37.67 Years (452 Months)

Month MTMIR Goal First Achieved

Figure 23

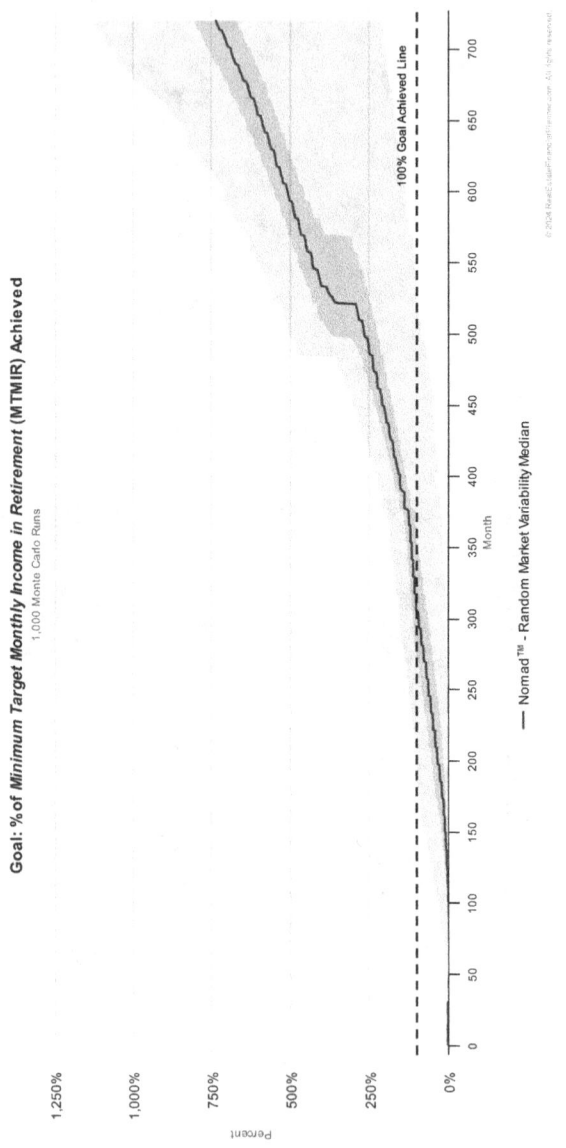

Goal: % of *Minimum Target Monthly Income in Retirement* (MTMIR) Achieved

1,000 Monte Carlo Runs

Figure 24

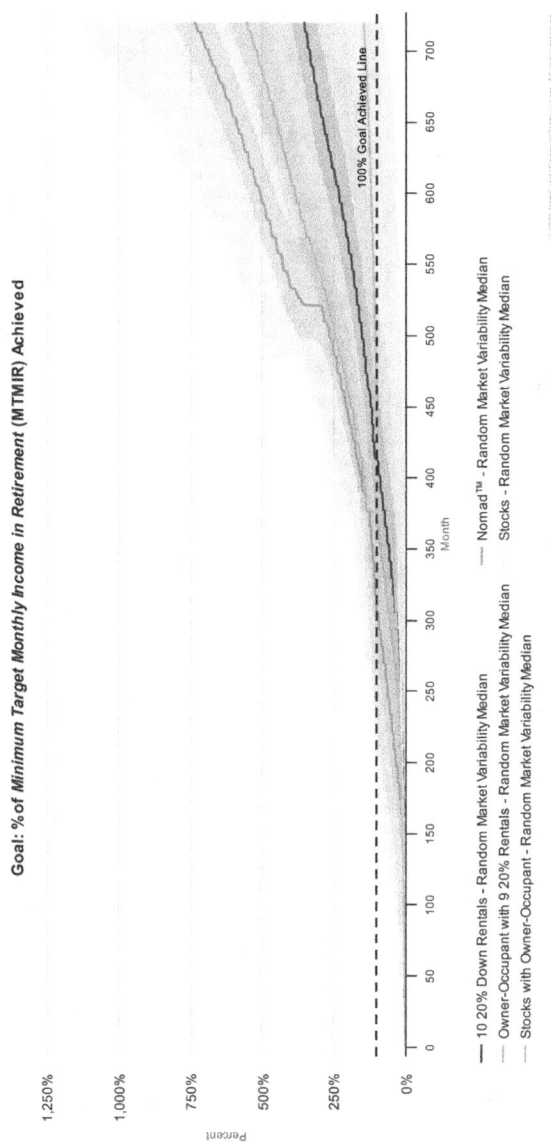

Figure 25

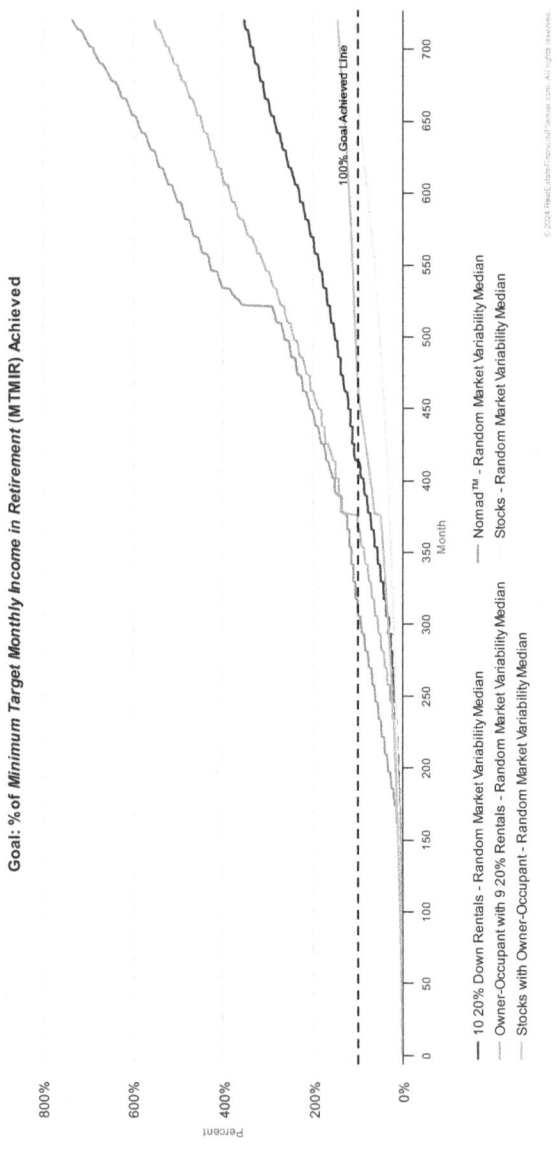

Figure 26

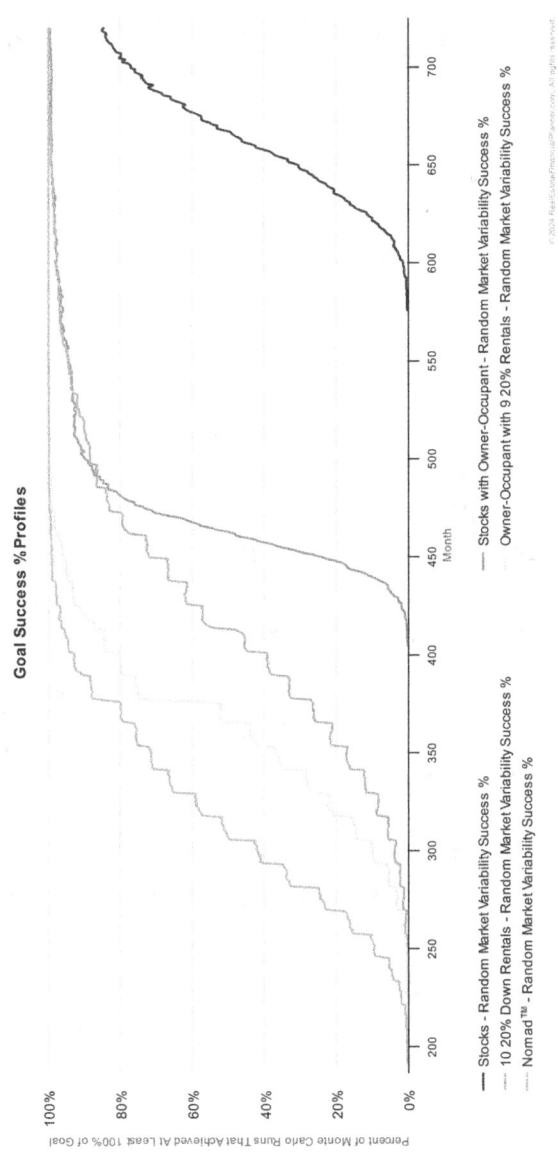

Figure 27

About the Author

James Orr is a seasoned real estate investor and the visionary creator of the Real Estate Financial Planner™ software. With a passion for sharing his wealth of knowledge, James has authored numerous books on real estate investing, covering a wide array of topics to help both novice and experienced investors succeed.

Living in Loveland, Colorado, James enjoys a fulfilling life with his wife, Tammy, whom he has been happily married to since 1995. Together, they have raised two grown sons. When he's not writing or managing his real estate investments, James is dedicated to teaching others the secrets of financial independence through smart property investments.

Also by James Orr

- The Real Estate Investing Mentor series of topic books
- How to Achieve Financial Independence and Live Your Passion Regardless of Age or Income: 10 Paths to Financial Independence Analyzed
- How to Acquire a Multi-Million Dollar Real Estate Portfolio With Just $3,000
- How to Acquire a Multi-Million Dollar Real Estate Portfolio Earning Just $5,000 Per Month
- Nomad™
- Ultimate Nomad™ Checklist
- Northern Colorado Real Estate Advisor
- Acquiring a Portfolio of Cash Flowing Properties In Northern Colorado: A Real Estate Financial Planner™ Blueprint
- Real Estate Investing Systems

Software and Spreadsheets

- Real Estate Financial Planner™ software
- The World's Greatest Real Estate Deal Analysis Spreadsheet™
- Should I Sell My Rental Property Spreadsheet™
- Should I Refinance My Rental Property Spreadsheet™
- CapEx Estimator for Rental Property – Basic and Advanced Spreadsheets
- Financial Independence Asset Allocation and Cash Flow Engines Spreadsheet™
- The Investor's Agent One-Page Business Plan™

A Small Request

Thank you for reading *The Real Estate Investing Mentor: The Affordable $50K Coaching Alternative* topic book on **Introduction to House Hacking Real Estate Investing**.

I am positive if you follow what I've written, you will be on your way to successfully investing in real estate. When you do please reach out and share your story.

I have a small, quick favor to ask. Would you mind taking a minute or two and leaving an honest review for this book on Amazon?

Reviews are the BEST way to help others purchase this book and keep the price of my books low for everyone, and I check all my reviews looking for helpful feedback.

Please visit:

https://REFP.info/intro-house-hack-book

Questions?

Thank you for taking the time to read this book. If a concept sparked a question or if you feel there's an area that could be explained more clearly, I'd truly appreciate hearing from you. You can reach me at **jamesorr@gmail.com** with any feedback specific to this title. My goal is to make each book as helpful and practical as possible, and your input plays a big part in that.

Just a note—while I'm here to help deepen your understanding of this book's topics, this isn't intended as a personal coaching service. For advice tailored to your own situation, I encourage you to work closely with a real estate agent who can provide the insight and support unique to your goals.

Thank you again for reading, and for helping me make this series an even better resource for investors like you.

www.ingramcontent.com/pod-product-compliance
Lightning Source LLC
Chambersburg PA
CBHW071507220526
45472CB00003B/941